SPORT COMPETITION ANXIETY TEST

D0870275

RAINER MARTENS
University of Illinois

HUMAN KINETICS PUBLISHERS
Box 5076
Champaign, Illinois   61820

Cover design: Susan Lieburn

Second Printing, 1982

PREFACE

People get anxious when they compete in sports, some more than others. In this monograph, I describe the development of an instrument that identifies those persons who become more or less anxious in competitive sport situations. Known as the Sport Competition Anxiety Test (SCAT), this instrument measures competitive trait anxiety. The theoretical basis used to develop the test is described in detail in the first three chapters. The actual test construction procedures are presented in Chapters 4 and 5; the child and adult forms of SCAT are reproduced and instructions for using SCAT are given in Chapter 6. Chapter 7 was included to assist researchers in determining methods for measuring state anxiety.

SCAT is a psychological tool developed especially for sports. In this monograph, compelling evidence is presented indicating that SCAT, a sport-specific trait anxiety inventory, is a superior predictor of state anxiety when compared with general trait anxiety inventories. These results have strengthened my conviction that sport psychologists need to develop sport-specific constructs and instruments to measure these constructs in order to better understand human behavior in sport contexts.

While normally a preface outlines what is included in a book, in this preface I want to mention what has not been included. At one time I had intended to present a theory of competitive stress which I have been working on for several years. The theory's evolution, however, has been slow. As so often is the case, what appeared to be a simple, but powerful, explanatory theory has become increasingly complex as the theory evolved. As this monograph goes to press I have not yet resolved some of the ambiguities in the theory to my satisfaction, and thus do not refer to it here.

Obviously, an instrument such as SCAT is of little value unless it is put to use. I am hopeful that it will be, but one caution is needed. In using SCAT, as with any psychological inventory, it is easy to haphazardly obtain responses. In developing SCAT, we always sought to create an atmosphere that conveyed to subjects the importance of honest responses and the significance of subjects' contribution to our research. As a result I believe that we obtained minimum distortion in respondents' answers. To obtain reliable results this same atmosphere is needed.

As fellow researchers use SCAT, please inform me of your findings. In this way I will be able to monitor the use of SCAT and will be able to keep the monograph updated.

I want to acknowledge the cooperation of thousands of subjects who willingly gave their time to assist in the development of SCAT. During the last five years that I have been working on this instrument, I have been fortunate to have the assistance of some splendid people. My sincere thanks go to Charles Giambrone, Dan and Donna Landers, William McElmurry, Karl Newell, Eldon Partridge, James Peterson, and my wife, Marilyn, who assisted in collecting data during different phases of SCAT's development. I particularly want to recognize the contributions of my three research associates—Diane Gill, Tara Scanlan, and Julie Simon—who worked many hours on this project over the last few years. Not only did they contribute by performing the routine tasks involved they contributed creatively to the research reported in Chapter 5. More importantly they contributed willingly and enthusiastically and their involvement made this project enjoyable when it sometimes became a trifle tedious. Dan Landers and E. Dean Ryan made many valuable suggestions on an earlier draft of the manuscript. I thank them both. Finally, I thank Marilyn who has given me time to work on this project and who, although reluctantly, came out of retirement to type the manuscript.

Rainer Martens
University of Illinois
August 1976

CONTENTS

CHAPTER 1

ANXIETY IN SPORT

Some years ago through an odd set of occurrences I found myself coaching wrestling at the University of Montana. The team's 147 lb. wrestler (I will fictitiously name him Jim Macey) was a young man with great ability. In fact, Jim knew considerably more about wrestling than I, although he never shoved that fact in my face. Jim's teammates admired his talent and early in the season elected him team captain.

Our first meet of the season was at Eastern Washington State University in Cheney. After weighing in and seeing Jim's opponent, I was confident that he would have little difficulty winning. One to two hours before the meet, however, I noticed that Jim was very quiet and not his usual smiling, loquacious self. I inquired if he were feeling ill, but he assured me he was not.

That evening we defeated Eastern Washington 26-20 giving our team its first victory of the season and my first win as a head coach. But the win was not totally satisfying. Jim won his bout, but by a narrow margin. He wrestled as if he were a different person. Nonaggressive throughout the bout, Jim permitted his opponent "to take the bout to him". Rather than Jim wrestling his usual aggressive, offensive style, he was defensive. It was only his superior skills and a weak opponent that permitted him to eke out a 5-4 win. For several hours after the match he remained quiet and atypically withdrawn. I sensed that he sensed his teammates' and coach's bewilderment as to why he did not "mop up" his opponent.

As the season progressed I came to know Jim Macey much better. He became incredibly "uptight" prior to every bout regardless of how easy or difficult his opposition was. Jim was not enjoying wrestling because of this enormous competitive stress and about midway through the season indicated his desire to quit. After several lengthy conversations I convinced Jim to stay with the team although in retrospect, I am not sure it was the correct thing to do. At the time I was convinced the team needed him and he would be an excellent wrestler if he could overcome his anxieties. I recall talking at length with him about anxiety; I could easily relate and empathize with Jim because I had also experienced high states of anxiety when I wrestled. While I always believed that these high states of anxiety helped me wrestle better, in Jim's case, it was unquestionably detrimental. Through conversations with Jim I sought to remove the pressure that he felt, but I could not since it was self-imposed. Jim, I felt, feared failure so much that he almost panicked prior to and during a bout. He could not get control of his emotional state as he approached competition.

Although I wanted to help, as a young coach I simply did not know what to do. I did not understand Jim's problem well, nor did I have a clear conception of what to do to alleviate his extraordinary high state anxiety. Jim never overcame his competitive anxiety and completed the season with a mediocre record, far poorer than his ability would have predicted.

My inability to help Jim and my frustration from a number of related experiences in sport led me to an interest in the then obscure field of sport psychology. I believed then and today that what is "in the head" is just as important, if not more so, than the physical skills of the athlete in determining a winner and in having competitive sports be an enjoyable experience. Consequently, I terminated a short coaching career to pursue my curiosities about the psychology of sport.

Because of the Jim Macey's of the world, sport psychologists need to answer such questions as: What causes athletes to become uptight? Why do some athletes "rise to the occasion" in intense competition while others "buckle under the pressure"? What are the short- and long-term effects of competitive stress? How does competitive anxiety effect the performance of the athlete? Can athletes learn to control their emotional states and will this help them optimize their performance? What can be done to alleviate hyper-anxious states? What can be done to prevent athletes from "burning out" as a result of the tremendous psychological stress from intense competition over extended periods of time?

Even though our progress to date in answering these questions and in understanding competitive anxiety is minimal, the horizon is brighter. Because of the proclivity of anxiety in sport, sport psychologists are seeking to identify the sources of anxiety and to learn how different individuals perceive these sources. With an improved understanding of the causes of competitive anxiety, sport psychologists are beginning to examine the mechanisms that athletes use to cope with competitive anxiety and the consequences of the inability to cope with it. Currently, some of the techniques being studied to alleviate hyper-anxious states include hypnosis (Morgan, 1972a), various behavior therapies (Wenrich, 1970; Wolpe & Lazarus, 1966), including a relatively new technique called visuo-motor behavior rehearsal (Suinn, Note 1), and psychotropic drugs (Wittenborn, 1966). Additionally, a number of different methods of relaxation training are now popular with athletes and are just beginning to be investigated by sport psychologists. These techniques include autogenic training, yoga, zen and transcendental meditation.

To discuss anxiety in competitive sport we need to establish a common language in order to communicate precisely and efficiently. Thus, at this point some definitions are interjected.

When a student undertakes the study of a physical or biological science he usually encounters a completely new vocabulary—i.e., new nomenclature describing new phenomena. However, when studying a social science, a student must frequently learn new meanings to nomenclature that he already knows. That is, familiar terms are given precise meaning to describe specific phenomena. Learning new definitions to familiar nomenclature seems to frustrate students more than learning new definitions to unfamiliar nomenclature. For the student with a low frustration threshold it is recommended that this section be avoided. Anxiety, stress, arousal, and competition are all terms familiar to us. To communicate accurately, precise definitions for these complex phenomena must replace the vague, general meanings that these words have in our everyday vocabularies.

Trait Anxiety and State Anxiety

Confusion existed for some time as to whether certain instruments that measured anxiety assessed a general tendency to be anxious or immediate states of anxiety. Although there was some conceptual distinction emerging between trait and state anxiety in the 1950's, it was Spielberger (1966b) who clearly differentiated the two. *State anxiety* refers to an existing or immediate emotional state characterized by apprehension and tension. *Trait anxiety* is a predisposition to perceive certain situations as threatening and to respond to these situations with varying levels of state anxiety. In Spielberger's (1966b) words, "anxiety states are characterized by subjective, consciously perceived feelings of apprehension and tension, accompanied by or associated with activation or arousal of the autonomic nervous system" (p. 17). Trait anxiety, however, is "a motive or acquired behavioral disposition that predisposes an individual to perceive a wide range of objectively nondangerous circumstances as threatening and to respond to these with state anxiety reactions disproportionate in intensity to the magnitude of the objective danger" (p. 17). Persons high in trait anxiety either perceive more situations as threatening, or respond to threatening situations with more intense levels of state anxiety, or both. The following analogy, suggested by Spielberger, is useful in conceptualizing the difference between state and trait anxiety. State anxiety is to trait anxiety as kinetic energy is to potential energy. State anxiety is like kinetic energy; it is a reaction taking place now at some level of intensity. Trait anxiety is comparable to potential energy; a latent disposition for a reaction to occur if triggered by appropriate stimuli.

Arousal

State anxiety as defined is closely associated with the concept "arousal". *Arousal* refers to the intensity dimension of behavior—i.e., a state of the organism varying on a continuum from deep sleep to intense excitement. Other terms such as activation and energy mobilization have also been used to describe the same dimension. State anxiety, unlike arousal, refers to behavior along two dimensions, intensity and direction. The direction of state anxiety is negative; it is negative affect. High levels of state anxiety are unpleasant. Arousal refers only to the intensity dimension of behavior while state anxiety refers to both intensity and direction. State anxiety is arousal produced by the perception of danger. (For additional clarification of the arousal construct, see the article "Arousal and Motor Performance" reproduced in abridged form in the Appendix.)

Stress

As a psychological construct, stress has been one of the most ambiguous in the behavioral sciences. Stress has been defined as a stimulus, intervening, or response variable by different researchers. Stress is a precipitator as a stimulus variable, a mediator as an intervening variable, and a behavior as a response variable. From a different perspective, McGrath (1970) conceptualized stress as a process. According to McGrath, four events must be considered in studying stress as a social psychological process:

1. The physical or social environment that places some demand on the individual.
2. The individual's perception of the demand and the decision about how to respond to it.
3. The organism's actual response to the perceived demand.
4. The consequences resulting from the response.

McGrath defines stress as occurring when there is an imbalance between the *perceived* demand and the *perceived* response capability of the organism. Furthermore, the consequences must be *perceived* as important and it must be anticipated that failure to meet the demands will result in adverse consequences. Succinctly stated "stress has to do with a (perceived) substantial imbalance between demand and response capability, under conditions where failure to meet demand has important (perceived) consequences" (McGrath, 1970, p. 20). McGrath's stress process is illustrated in Figure 1.1.

OBJECTIVE DEMAND	→	IMBALANCE PERCEIVED BETWEEN DEMAND AND RESPONSE CAPABILITY	→	RESPONSE

Figure 1.1. Stress as a process described by McGrath (1970).

Spielberger's trait-state distinction of anxiety is easily conceptualized within McGrath's model. Trait anxiety is an important personality disposition that describes how a person is likely to perceive the environmental demand-response capability discrepancy. State anxiety on the other hand is a response to the perceived environmental demand-response capability discrepancy.

Note that in McGrath's definition of the stress process it is *not* stated that objective demand must exceed response capability; there must only be an imbalance. Normally we think of stress in terms of an overload—demands are made upon us and we are uncertain we can meet them adequately. Stress may occur, however, when the objective environment does not demand enough, when there is an underload rather than an overload. In recent years, a substantial body of literature has shown that stress-like effects may occur from sensory deprivation, social isolation, or stimulus impoverishment.

A somewhat different conceptualization of stress is presented by Spielberger (1972b). He describes *anxiety* as a process with the following temporally-ordered sequence of events: Stress → Perception of Danger → State Anxiety Reaction. Stress in Spielberger's model is limited to "the magnitude of objective danger that is associated with the stimulus properties of a given situation. In essence, we propose that the term stress be used exclusively to denote environmental conditions or circumstances that are characterized by some degree of objective physical or psychological danger" (p. 488). The individual's subjective appraisal of a situation as being physically or psychologically dangerous is labeled "threat" by Spielberger. Thus, Spielberger's process of anxiety may be restated as shown in Figure 1.2.

$$\text{STRESS} \rightarrow \text{THREAT} \rightarrow \text{STATE ANXIETY REACTION}$$

Figure 1.2. Spielberger's process of anxiety with stress being defined as a stimulus.

The significant differences between McGrath's and Spielberger's models are the terms they use for the processes they describe. Spielberger refers to his process as anxiety and McGrath to his as stress. In essence, they are describing the same process but Spielberger refers to it as anxiety while McGrath calls it stress. Spielberger uses the term stress as a stimulus; McGrath refers to the stimulus as the objective demand. Spielberger uses the succinct term threat to describe what McGrath calls an "imbalance perceived between demand and response capability."

While McGrath and Spielberger's models are in essence the same, I prefer the term stress rather than anxiety to describe the process. My preferences are twofold: (a) Anxiety is too often associated only with personality traits, only one part of the anxiety process as described by Spielberger, and (b) stress is often considered to be more than just a stimulus variable. Thus, in this monograph *stress* will refer to the entire process that is associated with the occurrence of state anxiety, not just the objective environment that elicits the perception of threat. When discussing these objective environmental conditions that may elicit the perceptions of threat, we will refer to them by more specific situational labels. For example, in subsequent discussions we will frequently refer to specific elements of the competitive situation as being an objective environmental condition. An objective environmental condition may or may not be perceived as dangerous or threatening.

Spielberger's definition of *threat*, however, cogently labels the perception of imbalance between perceived environmental demand and response capability and will be used to describe this perception. Thus, to obtain some consistency in terminology, the nomenclature attached to the stress process as shown in Figure 1.3 will be used hereafter.

OBJECTIVE DEMAND *(stimulus)*	→	THREAT *(mediator)*	→	STATE ANXIETY REACTION *(response)*

Figure 1.3. Nomenclature for the stress process used in this monograph.

Thus to recapitulate:

State Anxiety is an existing or current emotional state characterized by feelings of apprehension and tension and associated with activation of the organism. State anxiety is negative affect. Hereafter state anxiety will be abbreviated A-state.

Trait Anxiety is a predisposition to perceive certain environmental stimuli as threatening or nonthreatening and to respond to these stimuli with varying levels of A-state. Hereafter trait anxiety will be abbreviated A-trait.

Arousal describes a state of the organism varying on a continuum fro deep sleep to intense excitement.

Threat is the perception of physical or psychological danger. It is the perception of imbalance between environmental demand and response capability.

Stress is the process that involves the perception of a substantial imbalance between environmental demand and response capability, under conditions where failure to meet demand is perceived as having important consequences and is responded to with increased levels of A-state.

CHAPTER 2

SPORT ANXIETY RESEARCH
AS A PROLOGUE

Before proceeding with my approach to the study of anxiety in competitive sport, I will briefly review what other psychologists and sport psychologists have done to date. Most research pertaining to anxiety and sport is concerned with one of two questions: (a) How does A-trait and A-state affect performance? (b) How does sport affect A-trait and A-state? Considerable research has explored these two questions by one strategy or another.

In the first section of this chapter we review those studies that have compared various groups of sport participants to determine if they differ in general A-trait. If sport participants, for example, are higher in A-trait than nonparticipants, or if participants in one sport are higher than participants in another sport, sports psychologists will have a reliable basis for investigating parameters of the sport environment to establish what the causes are for higher A-traits. In the second section we review evidence about how sport affects *A-states*. The major question here has been how A-states change during the competitive process, particularly pre-game A-states. In the last section we review the research pertaining to the influence of A-trait and A-state on sport performance.

Trait Anxiety Among Sport Participants

The study of individual differences in anxiety responses to competitive situations has been an important segment of sport personality research. The most prevalent mode of research surveys two or more groups of individuals using a standardized personality inventory to assess differences in a number of personality traits. This approach, commonly referred to as the inventory approach, has been used to determine if athletes differ from nonathletes or if one type of athlete differs from another type—e.g., weight lifters vs. swimmers. In this research, anxiety has been a prominent trait in each of the standard personality inventories used.

Several good reviews are available which summarize the large number of studies using this approach. For example, Hardman (1973) compared A-trait among 42 different samples of athletes. A-trait was assessed in all studies by the Cattell 16 PF using the derived anxiety factor. These samples included athletes from 16 different sports, athletes from the United States and Great Britian, and athletes of superior and average skill. In almost all samples the athletes were men.

The data showed clearly that most athletes (32 of the 42 samples) were within the normal range of A-trait when compared with Cattell's norms. The major exceptions were several groups of club sportsmen from England who were more than one standard deviation above the mean in A-trait. The fact that these athletes were higher in A-trait is difficult to interpret because the British athletes were compared with American nonathlete norms rather than British nonathlete norms. Thus, it is impossible to know if the difference is a result of being an athlete or being British. The important conclusion arrived at by Hardman is that most athletes tend to have A-trait levels similar to the general population.

Close examination of the 42 samples reviewed by Hardman failed to reveal any differences between athletes participating in individual and team sports or between athletes participating in contact and noncontact sports. Hardman did suggest that superior athletes are less anxious than average-ability players, while displaying higher levels of A-trait than the population mean.

The question of whether superior athletes are lower or higher in A-trait than less skilled athletes is intriguing. For example, if we find that superior athletes are lower in A-trait, additional research may reveal that it is participation in sport (the success, the increase in skill) that causes lower A-traits. Or, it may be that only those individuals with initially lower A-traits are able to succeed in sport. Alternatively, it may be that there is a reciprocal cause and effect relationship between these two factors. A little success due to some inherited ability may initially lower A-trait, these lower levels of A-trait result in lower A-states which cause better performance, better performance continues to reduce A-traits, and so on. I am inclined to believe that such a reciprocal cause and effect relationship is a more plausible explanation than a unidirectional one.

At any rate, coaches and athletes often express a desire to know the cause of the possible relationship between A-trait and performance competence assuming that the relationship exists. What have sport psychologists found who have investigated this relationship? While Hardman suggested that top-class athletes are lower in A-trait, he had little evidence to support his observation. In an early study, Gold (1955) observed that college tennis players were lower in A-trait than professional players.

This appears to be in opposition to what Hardman suggested, but it is rather difficult to know what this study says about the relationship between competence and A-trait. It is my suspicion that the difference in skill between college tennis players and professional tennis players in the middle 1950's may have been minimal.

Perhaps the most persuasive evidence for the existence of a relationship between sport competence and A-trait comes from Ogilvie (1968) based on his review of the sport personality literature. He concluded that athletes, particularly superior athletes, have unique and identifiable personality profiles. Superior athletes are emotionally more stable, have lower levels of A-trait, and greater resistance to emotional stress. He did not qualify this for any specific sport or the sex of the participant. However, in reviewing essentially the same literature, or in some cases more recent literature Cooper (1969), Husman (1969), Johnson and Cofer (1974), Kroll (1970), Martens (1975a, 1975b), Morgan (1972b), and Rushall (Note 2) all failed to concur with Ogilvie. Each reviewer concluded that there were no consistent differences in A-trait among participants when compared with nonparticipants or among participants of different skill levels.

It is clear then that reliable differences in A-trait among athletes when compared to other athletes or nonathletes have not been obtained using the inventory approach. This is not only true for the personality disposition of A-trait, but other personality traits as well. It is also clear that researchers have not been able to find a reliable relationship between A-trait and the athlete's skill level.

A study abandoning the inventory approach provides us with probably the best descriptive data of differences in A-trait among athletes. Griffin (1971) administered Spielberger's Trait Anxiety Inventory (Spielberger, Gorsuch, & Luschene, 1970) to 682 females engaged in eight competitive sports, representing three different age groups. The mean scores for each sport and age group are presented in Table 1.

Table 1

Mean A-trait Scores for Women Athletes in Eight
Sports and Three Age Levels

Sport	Age in Years			
	12-13	16-17	19+	Mean
Gymnastics	38.7	42.4	39.6	40.2
Swimming	40.6	38.1	40.4	39.7
Volleyball	40.0	39.9	37.2	39.0
Track & Field	40.3	40.4	35.1	38.6
Softball	40.4	38.8	34.8	38.0
Tennis	------	38.1	37.2	37.7
Field Hockey	36.7	37.7	39.2	37.9
Basketball	36.5	38.5	34.9	36.6
Mean	39.0	39.2	37.3	38.5

Note. Based on data from Griffin (1971).

The differences in A-trait for the three age groups was significant at the .01 level, with the 19+ group being lower in A-
trait. This difference, however, was relatively small. A-trait
scores also differed significantly for the various sports. Female
gymnasts were highest in A-trait and female basketball players
were lowest in A-trait. These differences were also not large.
There was no apparent trend that individual or team sport athletes differed in A-trait.

While Griffin's study provides us with clear descriptive data
of differences in A-trait, these findings are limited to the samples tested. Further descriptive research that unambiguously
determines if there are differences in A-trait for various sport

groups is required. It is my speculation, based on Hardman and Griffin's findings, that if differences exist in *general* A-trait between athletes and nonathletes, they are minimal. *General A-trait* is a measure of the tendency to become aroused in a wide class of situations. It is difficult to explain why athletes should be higher or lower in A-trait than nonathletes for all types of situations. This, however, may not be true when considering a person's tendency to become anxious in competitive sports.

In other words, it is much more likely that athletes will differ from nonathletes in A-trait specific to competitive sports than in general A-trait. This concept of situation-specific competitive A-trait is developed in the next chapter.

Changes in State Anxiety During the Competitive Process

Our attention now turns to whether or not individuals actually change in A-state as they approach a competitive sport contest and if this change differs for persons high in A-trait as compared to those low in A-trait. Spielberger's trait-state theory of anxiety (1972a) predicts that high A-trait subjects manifest greater increases in A-state than low A-trait subjects when the situation is perceived as threatening.

In an exploratory study using the House-Tree-Person projective personality test, Johnson and Hutton (1955) investigated changes in what they termed "neurotic signs." Eight college wrestlers took the test prior to the wrestling season, 4-5 hours before the first match of the season, and the morning after the contest. Johnson and Hutton suggested that the wrestlers displayed increased "neurotic signs" right before the match and then returned to normal the day after the contest.

Morgan (1970) administered 3 forms of the IPAT 8-parallel-form anxiety test to 7 varsity wrestlers at the University of Missouri. The first test was given before the season began, a second 45-60 minutes prior to a match judged easy by the coach, and a third prior to a match judged difficult by the coach. Suprisingly, the pre-match anxiety scores were lower than the preseason scores, but there was no difference in anxiety scores between the easy and difficult matches. Subsequently, Morgan and Hammer (Note 3) tested wrestlers from four colleges with the same IPAT scale. The test was administed in the early part of the season, after the weigh-in in the state tournament (4 hours before competing), one hour before the first match, and 15-30 minutes after the tournament. Unlike Morgan's earlier study, increases in anxiety were observed one hour before the match and a considerable reduction in anxiety was noted after the tournament. In fact, the posttournament anxiety level was below the initial early-season level.

I avoided labeling the anxiety as being state or trait in the previous paragraph. In the two previous studies, it is apparent that the authors were seeking changes in A-state, not A-trait. Elsewhere (Martens, 1971) I have questioned the use of the IPAT anxiety scale as a method for measuring changes in A-state. Schierer and Cattell (1960) refer to the IPAT 8-parallel-form anxiety battery as a measure of "free-floating, mainfest" anxiety. A content analysis of the battery indicates that the scales assess A-trait, not A-states and, therefore, it is difficult to know what the results of the two previous studies mean. A-trait is conceptualized as a stable personality disposition, not easily affected by specific situational factors. If in fact the IPAT scales measure A-trait, their test-retest reliability is poorly reflected in these two studies. If the scales measure A-state, it is not at all obvious from the content of the scales.

To clearly determine if competition causes changes in A-state, a scale that measures A-state unambiguously should be used. Better yet, to know if changes in A-state occur as a function of A-trait, scales specifically constructed for each of these purposes should be used. Klavora (1975) did this using Spielberger et. al.'s (1970) State-Trait Anxiety Inventory with 300 high school basketball and football players. The state scale was administered in a practice session at least 1 week prior to a game, 1/2 hour before a regular season game, and again 1/2 hour before a tournament play-off game. Unfortunately, several methodological problems, such as subject attrition, incomplete observations, and observations made under slightly different conditions, weakened this study. Hence, we must interpret Klavora's findings as suggestive rather than conclusive.

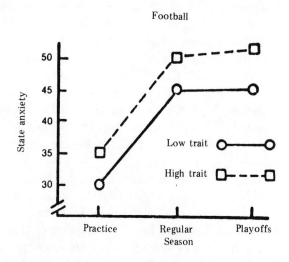

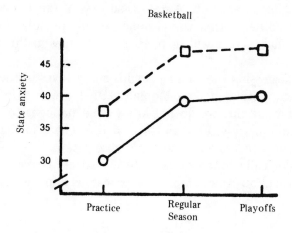

Figure 2.1. Klavora's (1975) state anxiety results for high and low trait anxious athletes participating in high school football and basketball. (Reproduced with permission from "Emotional arousal in athletics: new considerations." Mouvement: The Proceedings of the Canadian Psychomotor Learning and Sport Psychology Symposium, 1975, pp. 283.)

The results for both the basketball and football samples are shown in Figure 2.1. High A-trait players in both samples were higher in A-state for all three A-state measures. Both the high and low A-trait groups showed substantial increases in A-state just prior to both contests when compared to the practice A-state level. No difference was found between the regular season game and the playoff game. Klavora incorrectly concluded that these results supported Spielberger's Trait-State theory. To support the theory, high A-trait subjects need to manifest greater increases in pregame A-state levels than low A-trait subjects. Instead, both groups showed similar increases and dissimilar absolute levels of A-state.

Klavora's study raises some interesting questions, however, which need additional study under more controlled conditions. For example, why were there differences in A-state in the practice session between high and low A-trait groups? Does this mean the practice condition was also stressful? Or does this suggest that high A-trait subjects are chronically higher in A-state than low A-trait subjects, and regardless of the situation, they are always higher in absolute A-state than low A-trait persons? The issue of whether A-trait is a chronic variable or only responsive to situational factors will reappear several times in this monograph.

After discussing the findings of his study investigating prematch competitive anxiety, Morgan (1970) wrote, "Unfortunately, at this time, we do not know what happens to precompetition anxiety levels in the athlete." The evidence reviewed here concurs with Morgan's observation. The need for methodologically sound research to investigate changes in A-states throughout the competitive process is apparent from this review.

Anxiety Research and Sport Performance

Unquestionably, the major reason for the interest of coaches and sport participants in anxiety is to understand how it affects performance. A substantial amount of basic research has been done on this topic; but almost no applied research in sport contexts has been completed. The basic research has focused on the relationship between A-state and motor behavior or A-trait and motor behavior. Two theories have guided this research, Hull's drive theory and the popular inverted-U hypothesis. Although these theories are complex, they must be comprehended to understand the research investigating how anxiety influences motor behavior. In an earlier publication I reviewed these theories and critiqued the mass of research testing them when using motor tasks. This publication, titled "Arousal and Motor Performance," is reproduced in the Appendix in abridged form.

Two other articles are also reproduced in the Appendix to assist the reader in understanding the major theoretical issues pertinent to anxiety and motor behavior. Janet Taylor Spence, who developed the Taylor Manifest Anxiety Scale, took issue with two of the conclusions that I drew about drive theory and motor behavior. Her position is presented in the second abridged article titled, "What Can You Say About a Twenty-year Old Theory That Won't Die?" The third article was written by Charles Spielberger, also in reaction to my paper. This article, titled "Trait-State Anxiety and Motor Behavior," clarifies the relationship between drive theory and Spielberger's trait-state conception of anxiety.

At this juncture, we will turn our attention from the basic research on anxiety and motor behavior to current knowledge about the more applied issue of anxiety and sport performance. Each of us involved in sport has at one time or another speculated about the relationship between anxiety and sport performance, specifically A-state and sport performance. Most individuals believe that a little A-state is helpful; it prepares the athlete for the competition. Yet, I find almost unanimous agreement among sports experts that too much A-state is thought to be debilitating to performance. As one athlete said, "good performance is dependent upon being 'psyched up' for the contest, but not being 'psyched out'." These astute observations are the essence of the inverted-U hypothesis: Performance improves as A-state (or arousal) increases up to some optimal point, subsequently, additional increases in A-state are detrimental to performance.

Any sport aficionado will also tell you that individuals differ in their tendencies to manifest high levels of A-state in sport. This means that athletes differ in competitive A-trait and these differences in A-trait will result in two persons manifesting different levels of A-state in the same competitive situation. Thus, a specific competitive environment may be optimal for one person but not for another.

A sport aficionado also knows that optimal levels of A-state for one sport may not necessarily be the optimal level for another sport to achieve superior performance. Oxendine (1970), for example, suggested that football blocking and tackling and weight lifting require extremely high A-states; that basketball, boxing, and soccer require moderate A-states; and that archery, bowling, and golf require low A-states for optimal performance.

While these insights have heuristic value, they have minimal practical value for coaches and athletes with respect to improving an athlete's performance. It is not difficult to recognize when an athlete is at the extremes of the A-state continuum. Through a variety of behaviors, we know with some certainty when an athlete is not sufficiently "up" for the contest or is too "up" for the event. The real problem, however, is that we cannot tell with any degree of certainty a person's A-state when it falls between these extremes. It is seldom, indeed rare, that athletes are at the real extremes of the A-state continuum. Thus the athlete's concern, and that of his coach, is not with gross differences in A-state, but subtle differences that fall between these extremes. These more minute differences are not so easily discerned. Yet, the belief prevails that it is these subtle differences in A-state that often determine whether an athlete succeeds or fails in sport. The sport participant then is looking for a precise point, or perhaps a narrow band, on the A-state continuum that is optimal for performance in a specific sport.

For sport psychologists to provide the type of information that will be of practical value to the sport participant one major hurdle must be overcome—the measurement obstacle. The present crude measurement of A-state is unlikely to tell us much more than what a psychologically astute coach can observe. To understand how subtle differences in A-states influence sport performance, we must have instrumentation that permits us to reliably measure these subtle differences. At present we do not have sufficient means to do this (see Chapter 7 for an extended discussion of this issue). Only with more precise measurement of A-states will it be possible to determine accurately how small changes in A-state affect sport performance. With such measurement precision, it will be a much simpler task to discover effective means for changing A-states so that they are in the optimal range for maximal performance. Thus, it is my firm belief that little progress will be made in understanding how A-states affect sport performance until a major breakthrough occurs in the measurement of A-states.

At present then, sport psychology research has little it can contribute to the existing insights of coaches and athletes about the relationship between A-state and sport performance. Perhaps because of measurement deficiencies, little research has investigated how A-state influences sport performance in an actual sport context. Another reason that this type of investigation has not been completed is that the methodological problems of conducting such a field study are enormous, making this type of investigation difficult. Consequently, the literature pertinent to this section is limited to two field studies that are methodologically sound. One of the field studies was completed with little league baseball teams (Lowe, 1973) and the other involved sport parachutists (Fenz & Jones, 1972). Each study is reviewed in "Arousal and Motor Performance" in the Appendix. These studies, which support the inverted-U hypothesis, were only able to identify differences in sport performance when there were gross differences in A-state or arousal, and not the more common subtle differences.

The Past is Prologue

In summary, we know little except that our simplistic approaches of the past stand as a prologue to the future. While the problem of understanding the relationship between competitive anxiety and sport-related behavior is long from being solved, from our past research there is hope that better approaches and methods will yield the knowledge we seek.

We now turn our attention to the development of a situation-specific A-trait construct, competitive trait anxiety, and an instrument to measure it. Later, we will again examine the relationship between sport-related behavior and persons differing in competitive trait anxiety.

CHAPTER 3

COMPETITIVE TRAIT ANXIETY

Competitive trait anxiety is a situation-specific modification of the A-trait construct developed by Spielberger (1966b). *Competitive A-trait is defined as a tendency to perceive competitive situations as threatening and to respond to these situations with feelings of apprehension or tension.* The operationalization of the competitive A-trait construct is important in understanding behavior in sport, specifically understanding which competitive situations are perceived as threatening and how persons respond to this threat. The Sport Competition Anxiety Test (SCAT), discussed in Chapters 4-6, has been developed to assess competitive A-trait. The competitive

A-trait construct is based on four factors.

1. The recognition that the interaction paradigm for the study of personality is superior to the trait and situational paradigms.
2. The recognition that situation-specific A-trait instruments have superior predictive power when compared to general A-trait instruments.
3. The trait-state theory of anxiety which makes the distinction between A-trait and A-state.
4. The development of a conceptual model for the study of competition as a social process.

Each of these developments is discussed to explain what competitive A-trait means.

The Interaction Paradigm

Almost all sport personality research has used the trait approach. Some researchers explicitly select to do so but most implicitly do so as a result of borrowing a particular personality inventory such as the Cattell 16 PF, the Minnesota Multiphasic Personality Inventory, or the California Psychological Inventory. The trait approach is based on the assumption that personality traits, the fundamental units of personality, are relatively stable, consistent attributes that exert generalized causal effects on behavior. The trait approach considers the general source of behavioral variance to reside within the person, minimizing the role of situational or external environmental factors.

In reaction to the trait approach personologists have advocated a situational paradigm (Mischel, 1968, 1973). This paradigm asserts that personality should be studied by accounting for human behavior largely in terms of the situation in which it occurs. Situationism, however, is an extreme reaction to trait psychology. Trait psychology reifies internal structures to the neglect of the environment, while situationism hails the environment as the only important source of behavioral variance, neglecting individual differences. Both the trait and situational paradigms are limited views of the sources of behavioral variance. It is increasingly recognized among personologists that the interactional approach is superior (Bowers, 1973; Carson, 1969; Vale & Vale, 1969). The interactional paradigm, which has long been advocated by social psychologists and behavioral geneticists, views the situation and the person as co-determinants of behavior without specifying either as primary or subsidiary causes of behavior. Instead, the primacy of situation and person variables is dependent upon the sample of people studied and the particular situation they are in.

Kurt Lewin expressed this position in the 1940's in his now-famous equation, $B = f(P,E)$, where B = behavior, P = person, and E = environment. The situationist, in Lewin's terms, would prefer the equation $B = f(E)$, and the trait psychologists would prefer the equation $B = f(P)$.

While the differences in these three paradigms are hopefully clear, considerable confusion has arisen among some individuals over what interactionists are advocating. Those not converted to the interactional paradigm are puzzled as to why interactionists use the same traits in their research as the trait psychologist. The answer is that interactionists do not believe that traits such as A-trait, achievement motivation, and internal-external control are nonexistent. Quite the contrary, interactionists believe that traits are viable constructs, but that they are not the sole or even the primary determinants of behavior. Interactionists are not demanding the abolition of traits or the instruments used to assess traits; they consider these traits to function differently than do trait psychologists. Traits, or dispositions as interactionists would prefer to call them, are *tendencies* or *predispositions* to perceive or respond to certain classes of situations with certain behaviors.

To reiterate, trait psychologists view traits as having widespread influence on behavior with little or no concern for situational determinants—i.e., traits are the primary determinants of behavior. The interactionist considers these traits as dispositions or tendencies to behave in certain ways in certain classes of situations—i.e., traits are not necessarily the primary determinants of behavior. Atkinson's (1957) risk taking theory and Rotter's (1954) social learning theory, both interactional theories, are evidence of how interactionists incorporate traits or dispositions into their theories. Each of these theories contain both a dispositional construct (motive to achieve success or avoid failure in the former and internal-external control in the latter theory) and situational constructs (probability of success and incentive value of success in the former and expectancy of outcome in the latter theory).

The interactional paradigm then suggests research in which the behavioral effects of environment and individual difference variables (dispositions), and their interaction are concurrently studied. This paradigm dictates that treatments be applied not to random samples, but to subjects who differ on theoretically relevant dimensions. In the pages that follow, a case will be made as to why competitive A-trait is a theoretically relevant disposition.

General Anxiety vs. Situation-Specific Anxiety

Many behavioral scientists have examined the relationship between general A-trait and various behaviors, but they have not obtained the anticipated consistent findings and generalizations. A group of psychologists (Mandler & Sarason, 1952; Sarason, Davidson, Lighthall, Waite, & Ruebush, 1960) have presented an alternative viewpoint based on their belief that personology is not yet ready to study anxiety as a unitary, general phenomenon. Instead, they claim that anxiety is a learned response to situations. In other words, one person may become quite anxious when taking a math test, sitting in the dentist's chair, or delivering a speech, but not become anxious when competing in a hockey game, performing at a piano recital, or taking a driver's examination. Thus, we can better predict behavior when we have more knowledge of the specific situation and how persons tend to respond to these types of situations.

Mandler and Sarason, or the Yale Psychologists, as they were known, pursued this line of thinking in studying test anxiety in academic situations. Their research has shown improved behavioral prediction when knowing a person's situation-specific anxiety disposition and other relevant situational characteristics. As a result of these improved predictions, other behavioral scientists have also developed situation-specific anxiety scales. They include an audience anxiety scale (Paivio & Lambert, 1959), a fear of negative evaluation scale and a social avoidance and distress scale (Watson & Friend, 1969), and scales for measuring fear of snakes, heights, and darkness (Mellstrom, Cicala, & Zuckerman, 1976). After reviewing some of the research using situation-specific A-trait instruments, Spielberger (1972b) concluded, "In general, situation-specific trait anxiety measures are better predictors of elevations in A-state for a particular class of stress situations than are general A-trait measures" (p. 490).

The competitive A-trait construct is a situation-specific construct, especially developed to identify A-trait dispositions in competitive sport situations. Its development is based substantially on the evidence that situation-specific A-trait constructs are better predictors of behavior in the particular situation for which the construct was designed.

A Trait-State Theory of Anxiety

Spielberger's (1966b) conceptual distinction between A-trait and A-state, which was presented in Chapter 1, is fundamental to his theory of anxiety. The theory is illustrated in Figure 3.1.

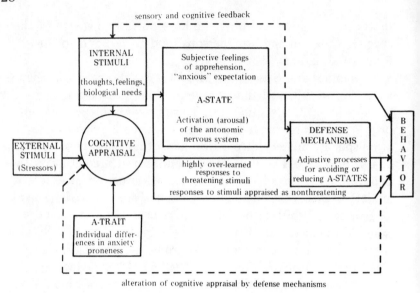

Figure 3.1. A trait-state conception of anxiety in which two anxiety concepts, A-trait and A-state, are posited and conceptually distinguished from the stimulus conditions which evoke A-state reactions and the defenses against A-states. It is hypothesized that the arousal of A-states involves a sequence of temporally ordered events in which a stimulus that is cognitively appraised as dangerous evokes an A-state reaction. This A-state reaction may then initiate a behavior sequence designed to avoid the danger situation, or it may evoke defensive maneuvers which alter the cognitive appraisal of the situation. Individual differences in A-trait determine the particular stimuli that are cognitively appraised as threatening. (Spielberger, 1966, p. 17; reproduced with permission.)

The Trait-State Theory of Anxiety (Spielberger, 1972a) is based on the following assumptions:

1. Stimuli either external or internal to the person that are perceived as threatening evoke A-state reactions. Through sensory and cognitive feedback mechanisms, high levels of A-state are experienced as unpleasant.

2. The greater the amount of threat perceived the more intense the A-state reaction.

3. The longer the person perceives threat the more enduring the A-state reaction.

4. High A-trait persons will perceive more situations as threatening and respond with more intense A-state reactions than low A-trait persons. Evidence indicates that situations involving potential failure or threats to self-esteem are more potent sources of threat than situations that are potentially physically harmful.

5. Elevated levels of A-state have stimulus and drive properties that may be manifested directly in behavior, or may serve to initiate psychological defenses that have been effective in reducing A-states in the past.

6. Stressful situations frequently encountered may cause an individual to develop specific psychological defense mechanisms that are designed to reduce or minimize A-state.

It is primarily through past experiences that some persons acquire high or low A-trait personality dispositions. From this theory it is clear that the focus of future research must be on the stimuli or antecedent conditions that evoke A-states, on the cognitive processes that interpret these stimuli as threatening, and on the behaviors that are manifested in response to the perceived threat.

The Competitive Process

So far, our attention has centered solely on anxiety, but our stated objective is to understand anxiety in competitive sport situations. To do so it is necessary to understand the elements involved in the competitive process. Elsewhere (Martens, 1975a) I have outlined a model of competition that specifies four components or elements. The four components of this model are briefly described below and discussed in relation to A-trait and A-state.

Objective Competitive Situation

The initial element of the model is the *objective competitive situation* which defines all the objective stimuli in the competitive process. It specifies what the task is, who the opponents are, what the physical elements of the environment are, and what the extrinsic rewards are. The objective competitive situation, in other words, specifies the environmental or objective demand. In the competitive process, the environmental demand is determined by what the person must do to obtain a favorable outcome when being compared to a standard. A standard may be another individual's performance (an opponent), an idealized performance level, or the person's own past performance. I have suggested elsewhere (Martens, 1976) that a competitive situation requires "[a situation] in which the comparison of an individual's performance is made with some standard in the presence of at least one other person who is aware of the criterion for comparison and can evaluate the comparison process" (p. 14). It is important to recognize that this definition specifies only the minimal requirements of an objective competitive situation.

Because the objective competitive situation defines the environmental demands for the person, it is this physical and social environment that may or may not contain sources of threat (perception of danger). The competitive process is an evaluative situation and most research concerned with the antecedents of A-state have found evaluative situations to be threatening. A number of writers have suggested that both the fear of failure and the fear of physical harm are two prevalent sources of A-state in competitive sports. Although Spielberger (1972a) has concluded that the former is more threatening than the latter, there is no empirical evidence to support this position. Within competitive sports, some of the specific elements of the objective competitive situation that may affect A-state include the nature of the competitive task, the ability of the self and the opponent(s), the available rewards, and the presence of significant others.

Subjective Competitive Situation

How the person perceives, accepts, and appraises the objective competitive situation is what I have termed the *subjective competitive situation.* The subjective competitive situation is mediated by such factors as personality dispositions, attitudes and abilities, and other intrapersonal factors. Most studies of the competitive process have assumed that the objective competitive situation is perceived identically by all individuals involved. Common sense suggests that this assumption is unfounded. To improve our understanding of how people behave in competitive situations, we must understand how they *perceive* the situation differently. Because the subjective competitive situation is an internal structure of the person, it can only be inferred from other behavioral indicators. Competitive A-trait is one factor hypothesized to affect the subjective competitive situation. That is, competitive A-trait is an indicator of a person's tendency to perceive objective competitive situations as threatening or nonthreatening.

Response

How a person responds to the objective competitive situation is largely determined by the subjective competitive situation. Individuals can respond at three levels: behavioral responses such as performing well at a task, physiological responses such as increased palmar sweating, and psychological responses such as increased A-state as measured by a psychological scale.

Consequences

The consequences of engaging in the competitive process may be self-imposed or acquired from others, they may be tangible or nontangible, and they may be perceived as rewards or punishments. In competition, the consequences are frequently viewed in terms of success and failure with success normally perceived as a positive consequence and failure as a negative consequence. The long-term consequences of competition have considerable influence on the subjective competitive situation, or how the person perceives future objective competitive situations. Understanding the history of consequences from participation in competitive situations helps determine whether a person appraoches or avoids them. In large part, the accumulated consequences of participation in the competitive process are thought to determine the individual differences in competitive A-trait.

Competitive Anxiety and the Competitive Process

The model of the competitive process is illustrated in Figure 3.2. It is not unlike McGrath's or Spielberger's models of stress or anxiety, (cf., Figure 3.2 with Figure 1.1 or 1.2). The model conceptualizes the popular Stimulus-Organism-Response paradigm in psychology but limits it to competition. In contrast to previous research on competition, the important feature of this model is the emphasis on the organism as a mediator between the stimulus and response. This general model may be adapted to the specific study of competitive anxiety as illustrated in Figure 3.3. Competitive A-trait is shown as an organismic variable (disposition) that is hypothesized to be an important mediator between the objective competitive situation and the A-state response.

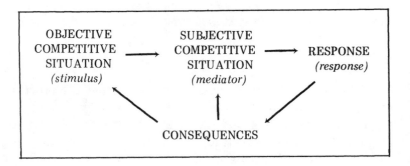

Figure 3.2. Martens' model of the competitive process.

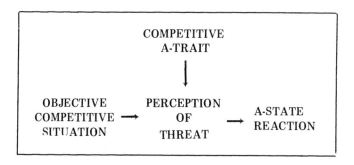

Figure 3.3. Competitive A-trait as a mediator between competitive stimulus and response.

Competitive A-trait must be inferred because it is a nonobservable construct. The usual research strategy for determining the viability of such an inference is to identify persons who differ on this construct through the use of a psychological inventory designed for this purpose. High and low competitive A-trait subjects are then placed into a competitive situation and their A-states are recorded. If reliable differences are observed in A-states between the high and low competitive A-trait subjects, support for this construct as a mediator between stimulus and response is obtained.

Additionally, our model needs to specify the type of objective environmental conditions for which competitive A-trait will act as a mediator of A-state reactions, a competitive environment as opposed to a noncompetitive environment. In a research study we may place one group of high competitive A-trait subjects in a competitive situation and another group in a noncompetitive situation. We would then do the same for low competitive A-trait subjects. These groups would create a 2 X 2 factorial design as illustrated in Figure 3.4.

We would predict that competitive A-trait would be an important mediator in the competitive situation but not in a noncompetitive situation. Thus, we may expect to find results of the form shown in Figure 3.5. In a noncompetitive situation

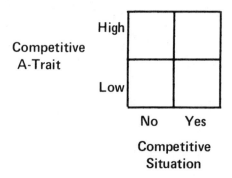

Competitive
A-Trait

Figure 3.4. Basic research design for investigating differences in A-state for low and high competitive A-trait subjects.

no difference is expected in A-state between low and high competitive A-trait persons; in a competitive situation high competitive A-trait persons will manifest higher levels of A-state than low competitive A-trait persons. (The reader may wish to compare these expected results to those obtained by Klavora [1975] in Figure 2.1).

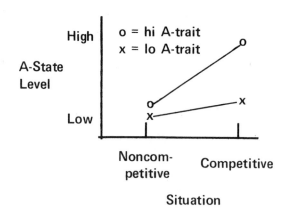

Figure 3.5. Basic prediction of differences in A-state for low and high competitive A-trait subjects in competitive and noncompetitive situations.

Much of what we will be discussing from now on will be based on this basic prediction. To investigate the importance of competitive A-trait, however, it is obvious that we need an instrument to assess this construct. The development of the Sport Competition Anxiety Test which measures competitive A-trait is described in detail in Chapters 4 and 5.

CHAPTER 4

DEVELOPMENT OF SCAT

Competitive A-trait is a construct that describes individual differences in the tendency to perceive competitive situations as threatening and to respond to these situations with A-state reactions of varying intensity. The Sport Competition Anxiety Test (SCAT) was developed for the purpose of providing a reliable and valid instrument for measuring competitive A-trait. In this chapter, I describe the development of SCAT, which follows closely the recommendations in the American Psychological Association's *Standards for Educational and Psychological Tests and Manuals* (American Psychological Association, 1974).

SCAT was initially developed for use with children between the ages of 10-15 years. Shortly after the initial steps were taken to develop SCAT, it was deemed desirable to develop an adult form of SCAT. After inspection of the inventory, only the instructions and one word in one question were modified for the adult form. The internal structure, reliability, and validity of SCAT were then determined independently for the child and adult forms. Instrument development involved testing over 2500 persons.

Planning the Inventory

The initial step in developing any inventory is to specify clearly what the inventory is to measure as stated in Chapter 3. The format of the inventory was based on several criteria that were thought desirable: (a) an objective rather than a projective scale, (b) a minimization of response bias, (c) an unambiguous procedure for taking the test, (d) a short time period to complete the scale, and (e) an easy method for scoring the responses. The format chosen for both the child and adult forms of SCAT was the one adopted by Spielberger (1973) for the State-Trait Anxiety Inventory for Children. The inventory is self-administered and each item has a three-point rating scale: (a) hardly-ever, (b) sometimes, and (c) often.

In planning the inventory format, the reactivity of assessing anxiety was a concern. To minimize this, the scale was not referred to as an anxiety scale and several spurious items were included in the inventory to direct some attention to other elements of competition. The format used for SCAT has been shown to be minimally affected by response sets when some of the test items are reversed (Smith, 1969; Spielberger et al., 1970). But, there is no procedure to eliminate the problem of response bias. No social desirability scale or lie scale were developed in conjunction with the test because these scales suffer from the same weakness that they supposedly detect.

Item Development

Two criteria were employed in developing a pool of test items for assessing competitive A-trait in sport. First, the item needed to be understood by persons that represented the population for which the inventory was constructed. Second, the item needed to have face validity for measuring competitive A-trait. Items for SCAT were developed by modifying items from Taylor's (1953) Manifest Anxiety Scale, Spielberger's (1973) STAIC, and Sarason et al.'s (1960) General Anxiety Scales. In addition, some items were developed by the author.

A total of 75 items formed the initial set of questions reviewed by six judges. They evaluated the face or content validity of each item and its clarity with respect to sentence structure. Each judge was given a concise statement of the purpose of the inventory to guide his evaluation of each proposed item. From the judges' evaluations, 21 items were retained, some slightly modified to eliminate ambiguity. The 21 items, along with 9 spurious items, were placed into the inventory format and instructions for subjects were developed.

Item Discrimination

This first inventory was labeled Version 1 and was administered in a group situation to 193 male junior high school students in three suburban Chicago schools. They ranged in age from 12-15 years and were largely from white, middle class families. Item analyses, triserial correlations, and discriminant function analyses were computed on these test results to determine item discrimination.

The item analyses were computed according to Magnusson's (1966) method for differences between extreme groups. The upper 27% and the lower 27% of the total score distribution were separated. This analysis compared the proportion of individuals at each extreme who answered the item consistent with the total test score classification with the proportion of individuals who answered the item opposite their total test score classification. The upper proportion ($N = 52$) was compared with the lower proportion ($N = 52$) on a nomograph to obtain the correlation coefficient between the items and the total test score. Those items with higher correlations were being answered consistent with the total test score classification.

The second analysis was a triserial correlation computed by procedures described by Jaspen (1946). A triserial correlation was used because one variable was continuous and the other was forced into a trichotomy (hardly ever, sometimes, often). Rather than selecting both the upper and lower 27% of the sample, the responses of all 193 subjects were used, with each item of Version 1 being correlated with the total test score for that respondent.

To determine the discriminating power of each item, when taking into account the correlation between items, a discriminant function analysis was computed between the two extremes of the total sample tested. The upper 33% and the lower 33% of the total score distribution were selected to represent, respectively, the high A-trait and low A-trait respondents.

The results of these analyses yielded fairly consistent patterns for each item. Based on the coefficients obtained, criteria for final acceptance of a test item were established. Each item had to have a correlation coefficient of at least .40 for both the high and low scoring respondents. This criterion is somewhat more rigorous than the .20 or .30 that is frequently accepted. Applying the criterion to both the low and high samples equally assured that each item was sensitive to measuring both extremes of the disposition, a characteristic absent in many other tests. The triserial correlation coefficient also had to be a minimum of .40 for acceptance of an item, and the discriminant function coefficient criterion was .90.

Ten of the 21 items met all these criteria and 4 others met 3 of the 4. For these 14 accepted items, the mean correlation coefficient on the item analyses was .65 for the high competitive A-trait respondents and .54 for the low competitive A-trait respondents. The mean coefficient for the triserial correlation was .61; for the discriminant function analysis it was 1.64.

Version 2 of SCAT consisted of the 14 accepted test items along with 7 spurious items. Version 2 was administered to two samples: (a) junior high school males living in Brockport, New York, and (b) male junior high school students in suburban Chicago. The same analyses were computed for the combined samples responding to Version 2 (N = 175). From these analyses 10 items were accepted, meeting all criteria except for two items having lower discriminant function coefficients. The mean coefficient for the 10 accepted items for the high competitive A-trait respondents was .64 for the item analysis. The mean triserial correlation coefficient was .68 and the mean discriminant function coefficient was 1.39.

The 10 accepted items from Version 2, along with 5 spurious items, constituted Version 3. Version 3 was administered to two more samples: to 106 male and female fifth and sixth grade students (ages 10-13) in Hutchinson, Kansas, and to 98 male and female junior high school students (ages 12-15) in the same city. Analyses identical to those performed for Versions 1 and 2 were repeated separately for each sample.

The results of the analyses for the two samples responding to Version 3 are summarized in Table 2. All 10 items satisfied the criteria for acceptance; and when the mean coefficients for the accepted items are examined for Versions 1-3 combined (Table 2 also), it is clear that the items far exceed the normal levels of acceptance.

The analyses on Versions 1-3 of SCAT determined which items for the child form of SCAT (hereafter called SCAT-C) were most discriminating. With instructions modified for adults and with a change in one of the 10 items, Version 3 of SCAT became the adult form (hereafter called SCAT-A). Form A was given to 153 university male and female students for the purpose of determining item discriminability for this sample. All items exceeded the criteria specified earlier for item acceptance. Item analyses for the high competitive A-trait persons (upper

27%, N = 42) and the low competitive A-trait persons (lower 27%, N = 42) yielded a mean of .61 and .67, respectively, for the 10 items. For the modified item (number 8 on the inventory) the item analysis coefficient was .52 for the low competitive subjects and .57 for the high competitive A-trait subjects. The mean triserial correlation coefficient across the 10 items was .64 and the mean discriminant function coefficient was 1.01. These analyses indicate that the items for both forms of SCAT exceeded the normal criteria for discriminability.

Table 2

Mean Coefficients for Version 3 and All 10
Test Items Combined from Versions 1-3

Coefficient	5th-6th Graders $N = 106$ (Version 3)	Jr. High School $N = 98$ (Version 3)	Mean for 10 Accepted Items Summed Across (Versions 1-3)
Item Analysis			
High Competitive A-trait	.65	.48	.59
Low Competitive A-trait	.57	.79	.66
Triserial Correlation	.69	.68	.68
Discriminant Function Analysis	1.11	1.18	1.36

Reliability

Two methods of determining reliability were used. One procedure was the well-known test-retest method and the other was through the use of analysis of variance. Test-retest reliability for SCAT-C was determined for two age groups, 5th-6th graders and 8th-9th graders, and for both sexes. These samples were selected from the public schools of Champaign-Urbana, Illinois. Within these groups, subsamples were administered SCAT-C and retested at 4 different time intervals — 1 hour, 1 day, 1 week, and 1 month later. The results, summarized in Table 3, indicate that test-retest reliability (r = .77 for all samples combined) was well above the accepted criterion level, which usually is recognized to be between .60 and .70.

Table 3

Test-retest Reliability for Four Samples and Four Time Intervals for SCAT-C

Sample	One Hour Retest				One Day Retest				One Week Retest				One Month Retest			
	r	n	T_1	T_2	r	n	T_1	T_2	r	n	T_1	T_2	r	n	T_1	T_2
Grades 5 & 6																
Male	.90	35			.61	35			.74	31			.65	55		
M			18.89	18.86			18.89	18.20			18.97	18.94			17.69	18.51
SD			4.43	5.03			4.43	5.00			4.06	5.04			4.24	4.15
Female	.85	49			.71	43			.87	26			.73	29		
M			20.22	19.14			19.93	18.88			19.62	19.19			20.59	19.83
SD			4.72	4.51			3.97	4.61			4.41	4.53			3.60	4.33
Grades 8 & 9																
Male	.85	31			.78	39			.80	36			.66	37		
M			18.35	17.23			18.82	17.28			18.19	17.86			19.11	18.30
SD			5.32	5.00			4.15	4.41			4.34	4.64			4.58	4.22
Female	.93	38			.80	34			.57	34			.82	34		
M			20.47	20.21			21.44	21.24			22.44	21.38			18.76	18.00
SD			4.95	5.22			5.29	5.62			4.67	4.85			4.81	4.89
Combined r over samples	.88				.73				.75				.72			

Combined r over samples and time = .77

Table 4
Reliability Through Analysis of Variance for SCAT-C

Sample	1 Hr.	1 Day	1 Wk.	1 Mo.	Combined
5th - 6th graders					
Male	.81	.79	.71	.81	.78
Female	.80	.73	.79	.68	.75
8th - 9th graders					
Male	.89	.80	.83	.84	.84
Female	.87	.89	.87	.89	.88
Combined	.84	.80	.80	.80	.81

The test-retest reliability procedure always contains some unknown reactivity because the subjects invariably recall taking the test previously. This reactivity increases the error variance and affects the correlation coefficient. Thus, another means of computing reliability is through a procedure using analysis of variance that does not require a retest. Procedures outlined by Kerlinger (1964, pp. 435-436) were followed to calculate the variance between items on the inventory, the variance between individuals (V_{ind}), and the residual or error variance (V_e). The reliability coefficient was computed using the formula:

$$r_{tt} = \frac{V_{ind} - V_e}{V_{ind}}$$

Correlation coefficients for the same samples used to compute test-retest reliability, but using the analysis of variance procedure (using the data from the first test only) are summarized in Table 3. This procedure indicates that reliability ($r = .81$) for the combined samples was slightly better than the reliability coefficients obtained using the test-retest procedure. A reliability coefficient of .85 for SCAT-A was achieved using only the analysis of variance method on the same sample as used for the item analyses.

Internal Consistency

Internal consistency is concerned with the degree to which the items in SCAT are interrelated. Evidence of internal consistency is demonstrated in part by both the item analysis correlations and the triserial correlations which correlated each item with the total test score. These correlations were uniformly high for both high and low SCAT subjects across the various samples. A more direct means for determining the homogeneity of the test is to examine the interitem correlations. A homogeneous test indicates that the test is unidimensional; i.e., that the test measures only one disposition.

The results for the four samples on which internal consistency was computed for SCAT-C and two samples for SCAT-A are summarized in Table 5. The subjects providing the data for the computation of internal consistency for SCAT-A were undergraduate students from the University of Illinois and the four samples used for SCAT-C were the same subjects used in the item discrimination computations on Version 3. For each sample, a correlation matrix among the 10 items was calculated from which the mean interitem correlation coefficient was obtained. The Kuder-Richardson formula 20 was then applied to these statistics to obtain the internal consistency coefficient. It is clear from the results that both SCAT-A and SCAT-C have high internal consistency.

So far, so good! SCAT has item discriminability, reliability, and internal consistency. But now the important question of validity must be determined.

Content and Concurrent Validity

Pity must be expressed for the neophyte psychometrician when first encountering the world of test validation. If not completely boggled by the sheer quantity of validities, the definitional confusion between them will likely suffocate even the most persistent novice. Depending on the source,

Table 5
Internal Consistency for SCAT-A and SCAT-C

Sample	SCAT Form	N	Mean Interitem Correlation	K-R 20 Coefficient
5th - 6th graders, males & females from Kansas	C	98	.32	.96
7th - 9th graders, males & females from Kansas	C	105	.32	.95
5th - 9th graders, males from Illinois	C	299	.30	.95
5th - 9th graders, females from Illinois	C	287	.33	.96
University undergraduate females	A	121	.35	.97
University undergraduate males	A	147	.30	.95

it is *essential* to establish the content, face, discriminant, concurrent, convergent, essential, predictive, construct, classical, congruent, criterion, external, incremental, nomological, practical, structural, substantive, and trait validity for SCAT. Under the threat of suffocation, a validity sieve was employed from which we were able to reduce our validity concerns to four, namely content, concurrent, predictive, and construct validity. The fundamental purpose of this section is to provide evidence that SCAT measures what we purport it to measure. While we demonstrated in a previous section that SCAT was reliable, and reliability is essential for a test to be valid, reliability does not insure validity.

The content validity or face validity of SCAT is a matter of judgement about the representativeness of the items in SCAT for measuring competitive A-trait. As previously mentioned, in the initial construction of SCAT 75 items were modified for sport competition from standard A-trait scales or were developed by the author specifically for SCAT. Six judges assessed these 75 items for content validity and grammatical clarity. Each of the judges were qualified researchers in sport psychology or motor learning and had either conducted research on anxiety in sport or were known to be knowledgeable on this topic. The information presented to each expert included a concise statement of the purpose of the test (a summary of Chapter 3), a list of the 75 items to be rated for content validity on a 1-to-7 scale, and a yes-no response on the item's grammatical clarity. With two exceptions, only those items in which all judges rated the item as having high content validity (a score of 6 or 7 from each expert) and being grammatically clear were retained for further use. The two exceptions were items in which minor grammatical changes were made. Of the 10 items in SCAT-C, all received a mean rating of 6.5 or higher. The one modified item for SCAT-A was not content analyzed by the experts.

Concurrent validity is determined by correlating other personality constructs with SCAT. Certain constructs are expected to be positively correlated with SCAT, others negatively correlated, and still others are expected to be unrelated to SCAT. Concurrent validity was examined by correlating scores on SCAT-C with scores on the Children's Manifest Anxiety Scale Short Form (Levy, 1958), the General Anxiety Scale for Children (Sarason et al., 1960), and the Trait Anxiety Inventory for Children (Spielberger, 1973). Each correlation between SCAT and the other anxiety scales was obtained from separate samples. The concurrent validity for the adult scale was examined by correlating SCAT-A with the Trait Anxiety Inventory for Adults (Spielberger et al., 1970) using a sample of university undergraduate males and females.

What should be the expected relationship between SCAT and these general A-trait inventories? A situation-specific A-trait scale such as SCAT is expected to yield low to moderate positive correlation coefficients with nonspecific anxiety scales. High correlation coefficients between SCAT and general anxiety scales would indicate that SCAT was measuring the same anxiety as the general anxiety scales, thus SCAT would have no unique purpose. Correlation coefficients near zero would indicate that SCAT bore no relationship to general anxiety which would also question the validity of SCAT.

Table 6

Correlation Coefficients of SCAT With Other Anxiety Scales

Scale	Sample	Form	Anxiety Scale		SCAT		r
			M	SD	M	SD	
CMAS Short Form (N=95)	7th-9th grade males & females from Kansas	C	4.32	2.12	19.23	4.78	.28
General Anxiety Scale for Children (N=75)	7th-9th grade males from Chicago	C	21.29	6.47	18.51	5.48	.46
Trait Anxiety Inventory for Children (N=105)	7th-9th grade males & females from Kansas	C	42.64	6.12	18.10	4.57	.46
Trait Anxiety Inventory for Adults (N=153)	U. of Illinois under- grad males & females	A	43.81	5.91	20.92	5.55	.44

As shown in Table 6 all of the correlation coefficients were positive and in the low-to-moderate range. Given that the test-retest reliability of SCAT produced correlation coefficients of .70 to .80, and that *general* A-trait scales when correlated with each other yield correlation coefficients of .50 to .60, correlation coefficients of .28 to .46 between general A-trait scales and a sport-specific A-trait scale is clear support for the concurrent validity of SCAT-A and SCAT-C.

In order to determine SCAT's position in the constellation of other personality constructs, SCAT-A was correlated with other personality variables. In one study, SCAT and the Junior-Senior High School Personality Questionnaire (HSPQ, Cattell & Cattell, 1969) were given to both male and female high school students in Moline, Illinois. The correlation coefficients between SCAT-A and each of the 14 primary factors of the HSPQ were computed using the standard scores for each variable. Also the relationship between SCAT-A and the second order factor "Anxiety" (Q_{II}) was computed. The second-order factor was determined by multiplying the primary-order factors by the Q_{II} weightings provided by Cattell and Cattell (1969, p. 37). The Cattells define their anxiety factors clearly as A-trait and not as A-state.

The correlation coefficients between SCAT-A and HSPQ are given in Table 7. Two primary factors were moderately related with SCAT in a positive direction for both males and females. These factors were D and Q_4—D measuring excitability and Q_4 measuring tenseness. Both factors clearly contain elements of anxiety. Factor C had a moderate negative relationship with SCAT-A. Negative scores on Factor C identify persons who are affected by feelings, emotionally less stable, easily upset, and changeable; positive scores describe persons who are emotionally stable, mature, able to face reality, and calm. Factor H was also substantially correlated, but negatively with SCAT-A for males and only slightly negative for females. A negative value on Factor H indicates a shy, withdrawn person who is emotionally cautious and is quick to see danger. In contrast, a positive value on Factor H describes a person who is adventurous, responsive, friendly, impulsive, and not quick to see danger signals. The reverse scoring procedure for Factors C and H explain why the correlation coefficient is negative. Thus, those who score negatively on factors C and H are positively correlated with high competitive A-trait as measured by SCAT-A.

Factor O had a low but positive relationship with SCAT-A for males and a slightly higher relationship for females. The Cattells describe Factor O as assessing persons who are self-assured, placid, complacent, and serene versus those who are

Table 7
Relationship Between SCAT-A and the HSPQ

Factor	Label	Males (N = 58)			Females (N = 98)		
		M	SD	r	M	SD	r
Sizothymia-Affectothymia (reserved-warmhearted)	A	10.12	3.32	-0.15	10.03	3.12	-0.17
Intelligence	B	7.26	2.14	-0.04	7.47	1.49	0.10
Ego strength	C	10.59	3.46	-0.33	7.95	3.56	-0.41
Phlegmatic temperment-Excitability	D	8.76	3.31	0.36	10.12	3.11	0.30
Submissiveness-Dominant	E	10.78	2.82	-0.14	8.41	2.78	-0.16
Desurgency-Surgency	F	10.98	3.29	0.00	9.27	3.74	-0.16
Superego strength	G	9.79	3.51	-0.10	10.40	2.85	0.02
Threctia-Parmia (shy-bold)	H	10.17	3.14	-0.38	9.61	3.52	-0.07
Harria-Premsia (tough-tenderminded)	I	7.64	3.83	0.10	13.91	3.23	0.22
Zeppia-Coasthenia (zestful-reflective)	J	9.94	2.60	0.07	8.60	3.19	-0.09
Untroubled adequacy-Guilt proneness	O	8.78	2.94	0.15	9.38	3.12	0.23
Group dependency-Self sufficiency	Q_2	9.98	3.54	-0.03	9.27	3.47	0.05
Self sentiment (lax-exacting)	Q_3	8.79	2.99	-0.10	10.29	3.07	-0.05
Ergic tension (relaxed-tense)	Q_4	9.29	3.68	0.32	9.88	3.22	0.41
Anxiety-second order factor	Q_{II}			0.37			0.36
SCAT		19.53	4.14		21.64	5.19	

apprehensive, self-reproaching, insecure, worried, and troubled. Factor O then clearly contains elements of anxiety and it would not have been surprising if this factor had been more positively related to SCAT.

The second order anxiety factor (Q_{II}) was positively related to SCAT-A as well. Hence, each of the factors in the HSPQ that contained some element of anxiety correlated positively with SCAT-A, although the correlation coefficients were not as large as would be predicted. The remaining factors were unrelated to SCAT-A. In general, little difference was observed between the male and female samples in the relationship between SCAT-A and each factor on the HSPQ, with the exception of Factor H.

In another project, the relationship between SCAT and the following personality scales was determined: Social Avoidance and Distress scale (SAD), the Fear of Negative Evaluation scale (FNE), both developed by Watson and Friend (1969); and the internal-external control scale developed by Bialer (1961). SCAT-C and the internal-external control scale were given to a sample of junior high school students; SCAT-C, the FNE and the SAD were given to a second sample of junior high school students. All subjects were attending the public schools in the Moline, Illinois area. The correlation coefficients for SCAT-C and each of these personality tests are summarized in Table 8.

Table 8
Correlation Coefficients Between SCAT-C and Three Personality Dispositions

Personality Disposition	Male				Female			
	N	M	SD	r	N	M	SD	r
Fear of Negative Evaluation	50	13.92	4.88		43	16.95	6.53	
with SCAT-C		19.86	4.30	.10		21.20	4.38	.36
Social Avoidance and Distress	50	11.86	4.85		43	11.05	6.30	
with SCAT-C		19.86	4.30	.11		21.20	4.38	.46
Internal-External Control	41	38.17	2.33		49	38.08	2.59	
with SCAT-C		19.17	4.41	-.32		21.20	4.29	-.37

The SAD scale measures the tendency to avoid being with, talking, or personally interacting with other people. The FNE was defined as measuring "apprehension about others' evaluations, distress over their negative evaluations, avoidance of evaluative situations, and the expectations that others would evaluate oneself negatively" (Watson & Friend, 1969, p. 449). These two scales assess individuals' dispositions toward social situations that elicit anxiety. Thus, it was expected that these two scales would correlate low-to-moderately positive with SCAT-C. For both scales the results for females support this expectancy, but not for males. There is no apparent reason for the substantial discrepancy in relationships obtained for the male and female samples, particularly in light of the other correlations that were unaffected by sex.

Bialer's (1961) internal-external control scale for children was developed to measure the degree to which the child perceives he has control or responsibility for the outcome of events in his environment. Those high in internal control perceive that they are generally responsible for outcomes while those high in external control perceive this responsibility to be with others, or due to luck or chance. The relationship of SCAT-C with internal-external control was moderately negative, indicating that high SCAT persons tended to be more external and low SCAT persons tended to be more internal. This relationship is logical. Those persons not perceiving control over outcomes tend to become more anxious in competitive situations where uncertainty of outcomes is high. Those persons perceiving they have control over their environment are less anxious because they have some confidence that they can obtain a positive outcome.

The final concurrent validation undertaken was to determine the relationship between SCAT and achievement motivation. The Mehrabian (1968) achievement motivation scale was administered to four samples: male 9th and 10th graders; female 9th and 10th graders (both groups coming from the Moline, Illinois public schools); undergraduate males from the University of Illinois; and female athletes from five volleyball teams who participated in the 1974 Illinois intercollegiate volleyball tournament. The first 2 samples responded to SCAT-C; the latter samples to SCAT-A. Samples 1 and 3 completed the male version of the achievement motivation scale, samples 2 and 4 completed the female version. Persons scoring high on Mehrabian's achievement scale have a stronger motive to achieve relative to their motive to avoid failure, whereas low achievers have a stronger motive to avoid failure relative to their motive to achieve.

In applications of achievement motivation theory (Atkinson & Feather, 1966), Sarason's test anxiety scale has been used as an index of fear of failure. Because we would expect that test anxiety has a moderate relationship with competitive anxiety, it may be expected that persons scoring high on SCAT would show a significant relationship with low achievers as measured by Mehrabian's scale. This, however, theoretically is incorrect. The test anxiety scale measures only the strength of the motive to avoid failure and does not assess the strength of the motive to achieve success. Those persons scoring low in achievement motivation by Mehrabian's scale are both high in the fear of failure and low in the motive to achieve success, while persons high in achievement motivation are low in the fear of failure and high in the motive to achieve success. It is equally possible to be low or high in both dimensions of achievement motivation. The relationship that is expected from the fear of failure dimension is likely to be canceled by the relationship between the motive to achieve success. Hence, it is expected that resultant achievement motivation and SCAT will be unrelated.

The relationship as seen in Table 9 was very low for all 4 samples confirming our hypothesis. There is no indication that high competitive A-trait persons are more or less motivated to achieve than low competitive A-trait persons.

In summary, we have determined the relationship between SCAT and certain selected personality dispositions to understand how competitive A-trait fits into the constellation of other personality dispositions. With only minor exceptions, the hypothe-

Table 9

Correlation Coefficients Between SCAT and Achievement Motivation

Sample and SCAT Form	N	M	SD	r
Male 9th-10th graders with SCAT-C	66	103.20 19.97	16.30 4.31	0.15
Female 9th-10th graders with SCAT-C	50	101.80 20.30	13.20 4.28	0.02
Univ. undergrad. males with SCAT-A	155	109.06 19.64	13.45 4.38	-0.11
Female volleyball players with SCAT-A	52	104.04 20.27	12.46 4.41	-0.07

sized relationships were confirmed. SCAT was moderately related to general anxiety scales and SCAT was moderately related to those factors on the HSPQ which contain some dimension of anxiety. The relationships observed between SCAT and the FNE, SAD, internal-external control, and achievement motivation scales were as hypothesized with two exceptions. Both the FNE and SAD correlated very weakly with SCAT among males, as compared to a stronger relationship for females. No explanation is apparent for these differences.

CHAPTER 5

CONSTRUCT VALIDATION AND OTHER SCAT RESEARCH

Construct Validation Model

Item discriminability, internal consistency, reliability, content validity, and concurrent validity are all virtues possessed by SCAT. But one psychometric property remains unknown, and it happens to be the most important propperty. The question is whether SCAT really assesses competitive A-trait, the construct it assumes to assess, or does it assess something else. It is possible, although unlikely, that an inventory such as SCAT could possess all the psychometric properties listed above, but actually measure something other than competitive A-trait. Therefore, it is important to establish the *construct validity* of SCAT. Construct validity is determined by testing the adequacy of hypothesized relationships between the construct being validated and other constructs in the theoretical framework.

Therefore, it is necessary to show that SCAT predicts A-state in competitive situations in accordance with our theoretical expectations. The reader may recognize that such evidence of construct validity is simply predictive validity. There is, though, a subtle difference between construct and predictive validity. The model developed for the construct validation of SCAT, which is presented in Figure 5.1, will hopefully help to clarify this difference.

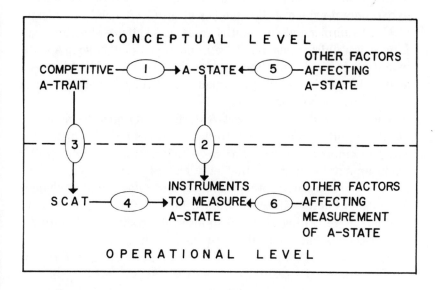

Figure 5.1. Construct validation model for SCAT.

The theoretical relationship between competitive A-trait and A-state is shown as Link 1 in Figure 5.1. As discussed in Chapter 3, the expected relationship is that persons high in competitive A-trait perceive more competitive situations as threatening and/or perceive greater degrees of threat in a competitive situation and hence respond with higher A-states. No difference in A-states between high and low competitive A-trait persons is predicted in noncompetitive situations.

To determine construct validity for SCAT, Link 3 is examined through the assessment of the relationship shown in Link 4. Predictive validity is represented by Link 4 (the operational level of Link 1) and construct validity is shown as Link 3 (the linkage between the theoretical construct and its operationalization). To the extent that Link 4 is supported (i.e., SCAT predicts A-states), it is possible to infer construct validity, assuming that Links 1 and 2 are valid and Links 5 and 6 are properly controlled. In any validation process it is necessary to assume that some links are valid while testing other links. In this model the assumption that Links 1 and 2 are valid is based on previous experimental evidence. Spielberger et al. (1970) and Spielberger (1972a) summarized substantial research evidence showing that Link 1 is valid for *general A-trait* and that Spielberger's A-state inventory is a valid method of assessing A-state (Link 2). It is assumed here that Link 1 is equally valid for competitive A-trait (see discussion in Chapter 3).

The factors shown to affect A-state and its measurement (Links 5 and 6) must be controlled or systematically manipulated in empirical testing. Factors affecting Link 5 include all environmental conditions that may change A-state such as the presence of evaluative others, failure, and unanticipated changes in routine. Factors affecting Link 6 include such measurement artifacts as recording errors, response sets, social desirability, acquiescence, and insensitivity of instrumentation.

Next, we will review both experimental and field studies that have examined the relationship between SCAT and A-state (Link 4). Although a complete report for several of these studies is available elsewhere, each is briefly reviewed here and combined with the unreported evidence in order to evaluate the total evidence for the construct validity of SCAT.

Experimental Studies

The first three studies assessing the construct validity of SCAT were carried out in laboratory-controlled conditions, but simulated a real-life competitive situation in such a way that subjects did not perceive the experiment as a laboratory experiment. The three experiments assessed the effects of competitive A-trait as well as the outcome of the competition (success-failure) on A-state. The main hypothesis of these studies was that high SCAT persons manifest higher A-states than low SCAT persons when in a stressful competitive situation. It also was hypothesized that higher A-states occur when failing than succeeding because failure is more threatening. The interaction between SCAT and success-failure was tested, but no hypothesis about the findings was proposed. Because SCAT is designed to predict A-states before competition and not after the competition, there was no basis for formulating a prediction about this interaction.

Study 1

Study 1 was conducted by Scanlan (1975) as a part of her doctoral dissertation. SCAT was administered several weeks prior to the experimental phase to 306 10-12 year old males. Forty-one subjects scoring in the upper quartile (high SCAT) and 42 subjects scoring in the lower quartile (low SCAT) on SCAT-C were selected and randomly assigned to one of the following three success-failure groups: (a) win 80% of the contests (W_{80}), (b) win 50% of the contests (W_{50}), and (c) win 20% of the contests (W_{20}). Thus the design of the study was a SCAT X Success-Failure (2 X 3) factorial. A-state was assessed by the Spielberger State Anxiety Inventory for Children (SAIC) and by the sudorimeter which assesses palmar sweating. The initial A-state assessment (basal measure) was made after an 8-minute rest period and prior to entering the testing area. A-state assessments were also made immediately prior to competition (precompetition), after competition (post-competition), and after the final debriefing (postdebriefing).

The experimental testing was conducted in a mobile van parked on the school site. Subjects competed on a complex motor maze for 20 contests with a bogus opponent at another school in a similar van via a purported computer hookup (see Figures 5.2-3). Success-failure was manipulated by the experimenter and evaluation potential was maximized through instructions, knowledge of results, and emphasis on the subject's ability as the primary determinant of the outcome. A condensed portion of the instructions provides some feel for the competitive atmosphere created for the subject.

> You will be competing with an opponent for 20 contests . . . We will 'hook up' with your opponent through the computer. The computer will send information about how you are doing to your opponent. It will also send information to you about how your opponent is doing. This information will be shown here by these lights. As you move the ball through the maze, this row of white lights will flash on . . . The first person to reach the finish will be the winner and his red winner light will flash on . . . .
>
> This is the computer that I was talking about. The computer will automatically record the winner and loser of each contest. The final results of the competition will be sent around to all of the testing areas on a computer print-out just like this one . . . Your name will be placed on a list just like this one . . . so that everyone will be able to see how well you did. That's why we would like to see you do well and be on the top of the list . . . This is also an excellent test of motor coordination and sports ability and that's another reason we would like to see you do well (Scanlan, 1975, pp. 110-112).

From the informal reports of experimenters and subjects, it appeared that this procedure for creating a competitive condition was quite effective. The subjects displayed many of the behavioral indicators of heightened A-states, such as restlessness, irregular speech patterns, and fidgetiness.

The data obtained in Study 1 were analyzed using difference scores in an analysis of variance. The difference score was computed by subtracting the basal A-state scores from each of the subsequent A-state scores. Although the SCAT main effect was not significant, the SCAT X A-state repeated tests interaction

Figure 5.2. Motor maze and subject console.

Figure 5.3. Experimenter control console.

was significant, $F(2, 156) = 4.88$, $p<.01$. The mean difference scores for the high and low SCAT subjects is given in Table 10. A positive score indicates an increase in A-state from the basal measure and a negative score indicates a decrease in A-state. High SCAT subjects had a larger increase in A-state than low SCAT subjects for the precompetition A-state score, but this difference was only marginally significant ($p<.10$). There was no significant differences between high and low SCAT subjects for the postcompetition difference score, but high SCAT subjects showed a greater reduction in A-state than low SCAT subjects for the postdebriefing A-state score at a marginal significance level ($p<.10$).

Table 10

Study 1: Mean Difference Scores for High and Low SCAT Subjects for Three A-state Measurements

SCAT Level	Precompetition	Postcompetition	Postdebriefing
Low	2.90	3.83	-3.95
High	5.43	5.07	-6.21

As was expected, the W_{20} subjects manifested greater increases in postcompetition A-state ($M = 9.85$) than did the W_{50} subjects ($M = 3.57$), who themselves manifested significantly greater increases in A-state than the W_{80} subjects ($M = .08$). In fact, the W_{80} subjects showed no increase in A-state when compared to their basal A-state score.

The palmar sweat print results were a disappointment because of the unreliable and troublesome use of the sudorimeter. This method was not found to be functional for several reasons: the equipment is expensive, the solution applied to the fingers is difficult to remove and appears to affect subsequent measurement, and the sudorimeter is inadequately built for repeated use.

Study 2

Study 2 (Martens & Gill, in press) was very similar to Study 1, but involved the addition of a sex factor and a fourth no competition control (NC) level added to the three success-failure conditions. The design was a Sex X SCAT X Success-Failure (2 X 2 X 4) factorial. Following similar procedures and using the same age group as in Study 1, SCAT-C was administered to 490 males and females with 45 male and 45 female high SCAT subjects and 45 male and 45 female low SCAT subjects being selected for further testing. An equal number of subjects of each sex were randomly assigned to the four success-failure groups. A-state was assessed by the SAIC and was initially measured at the same time as SCAT, which was several weeks before the experiment in a classroom. A-state was also taken immediately before competing (precompetition), after 10 contests (midcompetition), and during postcompetition. The remaining procedures were almost identical to those used in Study 1.

The data from Study 2 were analyzed using a multivariate analysis of covariance, with the initial A-state measure as the covariate and the three subsequent measures of A-state as the dependent variables. The results of this analysis indicated that the SCAT, $F(3,77)= 3.04$, $p<.04$, and success-failure, $F(9, 187.55)= 4.50$, $p<.0001$, main effects were significant across the pre-, mid-, and postcompetition measures of A-state. Univariate analyses of variance and discriminant function analysis showed the high SCAT subjects were higher in A-state than low SCAT subjects, particularly for the pre-and midcompetition A-states. The adjusted means for these conditions are presented in Table 11.

Table 11

Study 2: Adjusted Means for Low and High SCAT Subjects for Pre, Mid-and Postcompetition A-states

SCAT Level	Precompetition	Midcompetition	Postcompetition
Low	30.17	30.55	28.37
High	32.83	35.30	30.88

The success-failure results showed, for the mid- and postcompetition A-state scores, that as the number of losses increased A-state also increased. The adjusted means for these results are shown in Table 12. The sex main effect and the interactions were not significant.

Table 12

Study 2: Adjusted Means for the Success-Failure Conditions for the Pre-, Mid-, and Postcompetition A-state

Success-Failure Condition	Precompetition	Midcompetition	Postcompetition
W_{80}	31.51	30.31	25.97
W_{50}	31.45	35.08	28.79
W_{20}	32.09	37.12	35.87
NC	30.95	29.19	27.87

Study 3

As its primary purpose, Study 3 (Gill & Martens, Note 4) investigated the influence of task type and success-failure on motor performance, satisfaction, and causal attributions in *team* competition. The experiment, however, was planned so that additional evidence was obtained about the relationship between SCAT and A-state. The 96 fifth and sixth grade boys and girls were selected so that the full range of SCAT-C scores were equally represented among the sample. Each subject was paired with another subject of the same grade and sex and assigned to a task using either a conjunctive or disjunctive scoring system. In a conjunctive task the poorer score of the two partner's scores was selected as the team score; in a disjunctive task the better score of the two partners was selected. The 24 pairs assigned to each scoring system were then randomly assigned to one of three success-failure conditions: W_{80}, W_{20}, or NC control.

The experimental task was the same as in Studies 1 and 2, and the procedures were modified only slightly. Each member of the dyad team operated a separate maze with the knowledge that the better score would be used (disjunctive task) or the poorer score would be used (conjunctive task). The team was led to believe that they were competing with a similar team in another mobile van with whom they interfaced via the bogus computer. The team could monitor their own progress and the progress of the simulated opponents through the display panel above the motor maze (see Figure 5.2).

The results for the primary part of the study were not enlightening. Individual performance on the motor mazes was unaffected by either the scoring system or the success-failure manipulations. The results did show that the W_{20} teams were less satisfied with team performance and attributed outcomes to internal causes more than W_{80} or NC teams.

In Study 3, A-state was assessed four times: an initial pre-experimental measure, a precompetition measure, a midcompetition measure taken after half of the contests were completed, and a postcompetition measure. Multiple regression analyses were computed to determine the ability of SCAT along with sex, task type, and success-failure to predict the four A-state scores. The F ratio for regression was statistically significant for each of the four A-state scores. SCAT was the only significant predictor of A-state for the preexperimental measure and the precompetition measure. SCAT also significantly predicted the midcompetition score and somewhat surprisingly the postcompetition scores. As was expected, success-failure became a significant predictor of the midcompetition and postcompetition measures.

In order to directly compare the results of these three experiments, similar multiple regression analyses were computed for Studies 1 and 2. These results are summarized along with those of Study 3 in Table 13. The data in Table 13 provide the clearest indication of SCAT's ability to predict A-states at various points in the competitive process. The results of the multiple regression analyses in Study 2 were almost identical to those obtained in Study 3 for the SCAT and Success-Failure predictors. Study 1 found SCAT to be a significant predictor of

Table 13

Summary of Multiple Regression Results for Studies 1-3

Standardized Regression Coefficients	Dependent Variables											
	Initial			Precompetition			Midcompetition			Postcompetition		
	Exp. 1	2	3	Exp. 1	2	3	Exp. 1	2	3	Exp. 1	2	3
SCAT	.17	.42**	.42**	.27*	.45**	.49**	—	.33**	.42**	.16	.24**	.22*
Success-Failure	-.07	.02	-.02	-.02	.05	-.12	—	.31	.37**	.45	.46**	.55**
Sex	—	-.03	-.02	—	.10	.06	—	.27*	.02	—	.14	.03
Task Type	—	—	-.03	—	—	.02	—	—	.16	—	—	.08
Multiple R	.18	.42	.42	.27	.46	.51	—	.53	.57	.48	.54	.60
R^2	.03	.18	.18	.07	.21	.26	—	.28	.32	.23	.29	.36
F ratio	1.37	4.90**	4.96**	3.18*	6.18**	7.94**	—	8.92**	11.13**	11.88**	9.29**	12.55**
df	2/8	3/68	3/92	2/80	3/68	3/92	—	3/68	3/92	2/80	3/68	3/92

$*p < .05$
$**p < .01$

precompetitive A-states, but not for the initial or postcompetitive A-state measures. This regression coefficient of .27, although significant, was somewhat lower than those obtained in Studies 2 and 3, for this dependent variable.

Surprisingly, SCAT was a significant predictor of A-state in Studies 2 and 3 even before the subjects were placed into the competitive situation. This was unexpected because SCAT was developed to identify persons responsive to competitive threat. While it is important to note that SCAT predicted pre- and midcompetition A-state substantially better than the initial A-state, SCAT did predict significantly A-states in ostensibly a noncompetitive situation. Why this occurred in Studies 2 and 3 and not in Study 1 is unexplainable from the evidence at hand.

Further examination of Table 13 reveals that SCAT marginally predicted postcompetitive A-states in Studies 2 and 3, although to a much lesser extent than for the pre- and midcompetitive A-states. Our construct validity model did not predict that SCAT would predict postcompetitive A-states, so these findings need further explanation. One possibility is that the A-state created during the competition carries over into post-competition. In other words, the heightened precompetitive A-state leaves a residual A-state that is not completely dissipated immediately after competition. It is not uncommon for athletes to require several hours to "come down" after participating in a stressful competitive sport. The possible existence of residual A-state after competing warrants further investigation.

From Table 13 it also can be seen that success-failure became a more significant predictor of A-state as the subjects experienced continued success or continued failure. As indicated by the postcompetition dependent variable, success-failure was a good predictor of A-states. Of course, it is at this point that the subject has complete information about the degree of his success or failure.

While these results are evidence that SCAT has construct validity, the results are not ideal. The percent of common variance (R^2) among predictors and each criterion is not as substantial as might be desired. For the precompetitive and midcompetitive variables, the percent of common variance ranges from a low of 7% to a high of 32%. Although higher percents of common variance would be desirable, several reasons probably account for this particular range. First, while the studies succeeded in arousing competitive threat, undoubtedly this threat was not as great as in real-life competitive situations. For example, the mean A-state score just prior to competing for the three laboratory studies was 33.14 and for the three field studies reported next was 50.4.[1] Second, other factors in addition to the predictors used in these multiple regression analyses are likely to account for some of the A-state variance. Third, there is undoubtedly some unreliability in both SCAT and the SAIC that increases the error variance. All of these factors suppress the magnitude of the relationship among the predictors and the criteria. Recognizing that these other factors do suppress the percent of common variance, the fact that these relationships were found to be reliable is noteworthy support for the construct validity of SCAT.

Field Studies

Studies 1-3 were high in internal validity, but offered little evidence of the external validity for the relationship between SCAT and A-state in competitive situations. To determine the generalizability (external validity) of the relationship between

---

[1] This latter mean A-state score was computed by doubling the scale value of the A-state 2 score reported in Study 6 and then adding the mean A-state scores for precompetition in Studies 4 and 5 and dividing by 3. While this procedure may be unjustified for rigorous statistical analysis, these figures provide a representative comparison between field and laboratory studies.

SCAT and A-state, three field studies (Martens & Simon, Note 5) were completed with female volleyball players ($N = 52$), male students in boxing classes ($N = 115$), and with female basketball players ($N = 136$).

Studies 4 and 5

In Study 4 the subjects were members of five Illinois university volleyball teams who were competing at the state volleyball tournament. Spielberger et al.'s (1970) State Anxiety Inventory (SAI) was used to assess A-state. The initial A-state measure (basal A-state) and SCAT were administered to four of the five teams the evening before the tournament and the fifth team completed the same two scales on the morning of the competition. One precompetitive A-state measure (A-state 1) was obtained at courtside immediately prior to a game on the first day of the tournament competitive A-state measure (A-state 1) was obtained at courtside immediately prior to a game on the first day of the tournament when teams were engaged in preliminary play qualifying them for the final. A second precompetition measure (A-state 2) was obtained during the second day of the tournament immediately prior to either a quarter-final or semi-final match. of the boxing classes administered SCAT and the noncompetitive A-state measure (basal A-state) at the beginning of a regular class in which a film was shown. The course was conducted in a highly competitive context, where the outcome of the contest when students boxed with each other was an important factor in their grades. Precompetitive A-states were assessed immediately before these competitive bouts which ocurred near the end of the course.

Results from Study 4 are given in Table 14. The correlation coefficients were corrected for attenuation because the purpose of this study was to investigate the theoretical relationship between these variables—i.e., the construct validity of SCAT. The

Table 14

Study 4: Means and Correlation Coefficients for SCAT and A-state Scores

Measure	Mean	r with SCAT (corrected)
SCAT	20.27	
Basal A-state	41.06	.22
Precompetitive A-state 1	41.46	.28
Precompetitive A-state 2	42.79	.44**

**$p<.01$

correlations between SCAT and basal A-state and between SCAT and precompetitive A-state 1 were nonsignificant, but the correlation between SCAT and precompetitive A-state 2 was significant at the .01 level. Surprisingly, the actual A-states did not increase substantially from the basal A-state to precompetitive A-state 1 or 2. Comparison with norms reported by Spielberger et al. (1970) for college females indicated that the basal A-state mean of 41.06 was in the 75th percentile. This suggests that the players' A-states were already elevated 6-18 hrs. before the actual tournament competition, and did not increase noticeably immediately before the volleyball game.

In contrast, A-states observed in Study 5 increased substantially from A-state 1 to A-state 2 (see Table 15). The correlation between SCAT and A-state, however, increased only slightly from the basal A-state to the precompetitive A-state. The basal A-state measure was somewhat lower in Study 5 than in Study 4 and the boxing competition was more stressful for the cadets than was the volleyball competition for the female players. While the difference in noncompetitive and competitive A-state mean socres was substantial with the boxers, the relationship between SCAT and A-states was similar to that obtained for the volleyball players for precompetitive A-state 2. No explanation for these differences in results between Studies 4 and 5 were obvious, other than the differing samples and field conditions.

Although these studies significantly predicted competitive A-states, they showed that SCAT and the A-state scores did not share a substantial amount of common variance (approximately 16%).

Table 15
Study 5: Means and Correlation Coefficients for SCAT and A-state Scores

Measure	Mean	r with SCAT (corrected)
SCAT	21.56	
Basal A-state	37.48	.42**
Precompetitive A-state	52.70	.49**

**p<.01

Several subjects and the research assistants involved in Studies 4 and 5 reported that they felt that Spielberger's State Anxiety Inventory contained items that were not particularly applicable to competitive sport situations. After some initial analyses and comparisons with other instruments, the State Anxiety Inventory was modified. The items more sensitive to competitive situations were primarily identified through factor analyses and resulted in shortening the scale from 20 items to 10. A complete description of the procedures for shortening this scale is presented in Chapter 7.

Study 6

To determine if the measurement of A-state in competitive situations was partly responsible for the pattern of results obtained in Studies 4 and 5, Study 6 (Martens & Simon, Note 5) was conducted using the competitive short form of Spielberger et al.'s (1970) A-state scale. This study investigated the relationship between SCAT and A-states in competitive and noncompetitive situations among female interscholastic basketball players. The players completed the noncompetitive A-state measure (basal A-state) and SCAT in an after-school session at least three days prior to their next game. This procedure was an effort to obtain a better baseline or noncompetitive measure of A-state. The precompetitive A-state scores were obtained at courtside immediately prior to a regular season game.

The basketball players increased substantially in A-state from their basal score (M = 18.44) to their precompetitive A-state score (M = 27.96). Furthermore, the corrected-for-attenuation correlation coefficients for the SCAT A-state relationship showed a marked increase from A-state 1 (r = .28) to A-state 2 (r = .73). These results are excellent evidence for the construct validity of SCAT. SCAT was only moderately related to A-state in the non-competitive situation, but in the precompetitive situation SCAT was substantially related to precompetitive A-states, accounting for 53% of the A-state variance.

In summary, the overall results from the three samples were mixed in terms of the ability of SCAT to predict precompetitive A-state. Evidence from the basketball sample, using the competitive short form of the SAI and a better baseline or noncompetitive measure of A-state, yielded the strongest support for SCAT as a valid predictor of precompetitive A-state.

Study 7

Study 7 (Simon & Martens, 1977) was completed with the same nine interscholastic girls' basketball teams that were tested in Study 6. Throughout this monograph it has been hypothesized that high competitive A-trait persons, when compared with low competitive A-trait persons, perceive more competitive situations as threatening and/or are more threatened in a particular competitive situation. Hence, they manifest higher levels of A-state. The first purpose of this study was to investigate the A-state reactions of basketball players varying in competitive A-trait in competitive situations that vary in threat. The method used to vary the situations was an adaptation of the S-R inventory popularized by Endler, Hunt, and Rosenstein (1962). The S-R inventory approach has been used widely to determine the proportion of variance that is accounted for by the person, the situation, the mode of response, and the interactions among these variables.[2]

An S-R anxiety inventory for basketball was completed by all subjects after completing SCAT and Spielberger's Trait Anxiety Inventory as described in Study 6. The S-R inventory, presented in Table 16, contained 12 different situations that were intended to vary from nonthreatening to highly threatening conditions. Some items described a situation prior to competition, others during competition, and yet others after competition. In response to each situation, subjects completed the competitive short form of the SAI, indicating their perceived A-state level when in that situation. All of the situations were associated with playing basketball, but not all were competitive situations; that is, not all situations described a social comparison process involving the subject. Thus, it was expected that SCAT would predict A-state to a greater extent in competitively threatening situations. In addition, it was expected that SCAT would improve as a predictor of A-state as the competitive threat in the situation increased.

---

[2]Initially it was our intent to use the S-R inventory approach to analyze the proportion of variance accounted for by the differences in competitive A-trait (person), by the differences in 12 situations related to participating on a basketball team (situations), and the differences in A-state levels (response). As we and others pursued this approach, it became increasingly clear that the results of such variance partitioning are largely a function of what the investigator puts into the technique (Cartwright, 1975). The technique also is based on some complex statistical techniques that have dubious assumptions underlying them (Golding, 1975). For example, the investigator can create heterogeneous situations, select homogeneous subjects, and provide heterogeneous responses. The results will probably indicate that a large percent of the variance is accounted for by situations, responses, or perhaps the interaction of these two; and a low percent of the variance is accounted for by the persons. In turn, the investigator can select a heterogeneous sample but use homogeneous situations and response modes to obtain the opposite pattern of variance proportions. Recognizing that an investigator gets back only what he puts into this approach, we abandoned such fruitless research and pursued the two purposes stated above.

Table **16**

Study 7: S-R Anxiety Inventory of Basketball Situations

1. You are watching a basketball game between two schools with whom you will *not* be competing. How do you feel when watching this game?

2. You are getting dressed in the lockerroom for a practice session. How do you feel while you are getting dressed?

3. You have just scored the winning basket and the game is over. How do you feel at this very moment?

4. Your team is about to play a very weak opponent. They have won only one of eight games all season. How do you feel just before the game?

5. You are five minutes into the game and the other team calls a time out. You are playing very well and your team has a big lead. The other team appears to be disorganized and unmotivated. How do you feel during the time out?

6. You have traveled out of town for an important basketball game. You arrive at the motel the night before your game. How do you feel just before you prepare for bed that evening?

7. The coach, team, and you are watching a film of last week's basketball game. Your team won, but you did not play well, committing numerous mistakes. How do you feel as you watch the film with the coach and other members of the team?

8. In the practice sessions all week you have been battling for a starting position on the team. You are quite uncertain whether you will be in the starting line-up. It is the end of the last practice session prior to an important game and the coach is about to announce the starting line-up. How do you feel as you are waiting to hear the line-up?

9. Your team is about to play the most important game of the season. You are at center court waiting for the tip-off. How do you feel just before beginning this game?

10. It is five minutes before your game with the defending state champions who are visiting your school. They have not lost a game this year. How do you feel as you wait to play this team?

11. With ten seconds remaining in the game and your team ahead by one point, you double dribble. In your anger you throw the ball down in disgust and the official calls a technical foul. The other team not only makes the free throw, but when they get the ball out of bounds, they score a basket and as a result win the game. How do you feel immediately after this loss?

12. You are in the midst of a very close game. There are only two seconds left in the game and your team is behind by one point. You were fouled while getting off a shot and have been awarded two free throws. The other team calls a time out at this point. How do you feel during the time out?

The mean A-state score of all subjects for each of the 12 situations is reported in Table 17. Simple linear regressions, computed between SCAT and the A-state scores for each of the 12 situations, and the t tests to determine their significance are also given in Table 17.

All regressions were significant at the .05 level except for Situation 1. Of the 12 situations, Situation 1 was the least threatening; the subject is watching a basketball game between two schools against whom she will not be competing. Because there is no evaluation potential, this situation is not a competitive situation for the subject, and hence, SCAT was not a good predictor of A-state.

Although the A-state scores were analyzed as a continuous variable in the regression analysis, the scores were trichotomized for each situation in order to illustrate the pattern of differences between low, moderate, and high SCAT subjects. These differences are displayed in Figure 5.4.

The pattern of regression coefficients did not indicate that SCAT was a better predictor of A-states as the threat increased from Situation 1 to 12. For example, SCAT did not predict A-states nearly as well in Situation 11 as it did in Situations 4 or 9. While Situation 11 was highly threatening as indicated by the high A-state mean, it does not describe a situation where competitive evaluation is anticipated. Instead, this situation describes the potential negative consequences arising in a postcompetitive situation. Because SCAT was designed to predict A-states prior to and during competition rather than after competition, it is not surprising that the regression was only marginally significant. Situations 3

Table 17

Study 7: Means and Regression Equations for Predicting A-state from SCAT for the 12 Situations in the Basketball S-R Anxiety Inventory

Situation	A-state Mean	Regression Equation	t test
1	15.27	$Y = 11.99 + .14x$	1.85
2	19.04	$Y = 9.77 + .41x$	3.96***
3	21.69	$Y = 15.44 + .27x$	2.93**
4	22.04	$Y = 7.93 + .62x$	8.11***
5	22.18	$Y = 10.68 + .50x$	6.13***
6	24.86	$Y = 10.05 + .65x$	6.57***
7	26.68	$Y = 19.85 + .30x$	3.24**
8	31.21	$Y = 22.32 + .39x$	4.27***
9	31.48	$Y = 16.10 + .68x$	9.28***
10	32.57	$Y = 20.00 + .55x$	7.04***
11	33.04	$Y = 29.46 + .16x$	2.24*
12	34.15	$Y = 23.65 + .46x$	6.49***

*p<.05

**p<.01

***p<.001

and 7, which describe postcompetitive situations, also had lower regression coefficients and were less significant than the precompetitive and competitive situations. Situation 4 is another example indicating that SCAT was not a better predictor of A-states as the threat increased. In this situation, which was not highly threatening, SCAT made the second best prediction of A-states among the 12 situations. Situation 4 describes playing an anticipated weak opponent. Apparently this situation was minimally threatening to low SCAT subjects but it did elicit higher levels of A-state among subjects higher in SCAT.

Examination of the 8 situations describing competitive and precompetitive situations reveals that those situations occurring

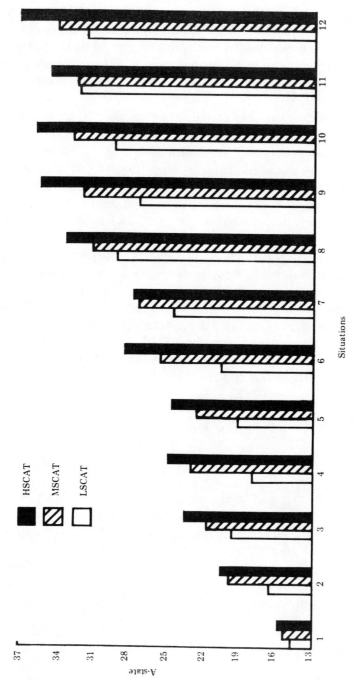

Figure 5.4. Study 7: Mean A-states for low, moderate, and high competitive A-trait basketball players for each of 12 basketball situations.

immediately prior to the beginning of the basketball game (4, 9, and 10) had the highest correlations between SCAT and A-state (r = .57, .63, and .52, respectively). Furthermore, as the other three precompetitive situations (2, 6, and 8) show, the magnitude of the correlations between SCAT and A-state decreased (r = .32, .49, and .35, respectively) as the time to compete neared.

It was somewhat unexpected, however, that SCAT did not improve as a predictor as A-states increased. Inspection of the mean A-state scores and the distribution of scores in each situation provide a possible explanation as to why this occurred. For the more threatening precompetitive and competitive situations (9, 10, and 12), a ceiling effect appears for the higher SCAT subjects, but moderate and low SCAT subjects continued to show A-state increases in each of these situations. Because the A-state scores of high SCAT subjects were likely being suppressed by this ceiling while lower SCAT subjects' scores were not, the correlation between SCAT and A-states in these more threatening situations was also suppressed. Although SCAT did not systematically improve as a predictor of A-states as threat increased, it is quite evident that SCAT is a better predictor of A-states in precompetitive and competitive situations than in postcompetitive situations.

Predicting Precompetitive A-state

Study 8

An additional way to determine the validity of SCAT is to compare SCAT with another measure of competitive A-trait to see which of the two predicts A-states better in competitive situations. In sport, the assessment of competitive A-trait is commonly done subjectively by the coach. Coaches are generally quite confident in their ability to evaluate player attributes, particularly an important factor such as A-trait. Thus, the correlation between SCAT and coaches' ratings of player competitive A-trait was examined (Martens & Simon, 1976). A moderately high correlation coefficient was expected which would provide further concurrent validity for SCAT.

Sixteen intercollegiate women's volleyball teams participating in the Illinois state tournament served as subjects. Subjects completed SCAT the first day of play during 10 minute testing sessions. That same day each coach was given a rating form for indicating how anxious each of her athletes generally becomes when competing. The correlation coefficients between SCAT and the coaches' ratings revealed great discrepancies among teams, with correlations ranging from -.57 to +.62. The correlation for all teams combined was +.14.

As a result of the inconsistent findings from the volleyball sample, further consideration was given to the process coaches used to rate their players as well as the context in which SCAT was completed by each team. Several coaches indicated that the question relating to the athletes' anxiety was unclear. The coaches suggested that a precise operational definition of competitive A-trait be provided. Another factor that may have affected both the players' and coaches' responses was the fact that the data were obtained in the midst of an important tournament. Because of tournament scheduling, both SCAT and the coaches' ratings were filled out at various times during the tournament, some during lengthy breaks, and some immediately after matches.

Based on the information from the volleyball sample, the coaches' rating form of competitive A-trait was modified and the context in which the athletes completed SCAT was changed. The second sample which compared SCAT to the coaches' rating of competitive A-trait was the same high school girls basketball teams investigated in Studies 6 and 7. All subjects also completed Spielbergers et al.'s (1970) Trait Anxiety Inventory (TAI) at the same time they completed SCAT, an important additional comparison not done with the volleyball sample. Thus, three different measures of A-trait (SCAT, TAI, and coaches' ratings) were obtained in order to compare the relationship among them and to determine how well each predicted the

the players' A-state in noncompetitive and competitive situations.

Subjects completed the two A-trait measures in after-school sessions while coaches completed the coaches' rating forms at the conclusion of the season. The interval between the time the players completed the A-trait scales and when the coaches completed their ratings was several weeks. Coaches were asked to respond by indicating their perception of the athletes' emotional state immediately prior to competing (competitive A-trait) based on their observations over the course of the season. The form used for the coaches' ratings is presented in Table 18.

Table 18
Study 8: Coaches' Rating Scale of Competitive A-trait

This athlete's general emotional state immediately before competing:

: 1 : 2 : 3 : 4 : 5 : 6 : 7 : 8 : 9 :

Very Much	Somewhat	Very Much
at ease		over excited
calm		tense
comfortable		jittery
secure		anxious
relaxed		nervous

Similar to the results from the volleyball data, low and nonsignificant correlations were obtained between the coaches' ratings and SCAT (see Figure 5.5). The TAI was not significantly related to the coaches' ratings either. The relationship between SCAT and the TAI was .44 which corroborated other SCAT concurrent validity studies.

Two explanations may be offered to account for the low correlations between the coaches' ratings and SCAT. First, SCAT may be a poor predictor of actual competitive A-state. Alternatively, the coaches may be inaccurate in their perceptions of the players' A-trait. To determine which explanation was correct, each measure of competitive A-trait was correlated with the players' actual A-state just prior to competition. It was hypothesized that SCAT would correlate highest with the players' A-state, the TAI would correlate somewhat lower and the coaches' ratings would correlate the lowest. This hypothesis was supported as illustrated in Figure 5.5. These correlation coefficients are uncorrected for attenuation because our interest was in the predictive power of each A-trait measure. When corrected for attenuation, the correlation coefficients rose by only .01.

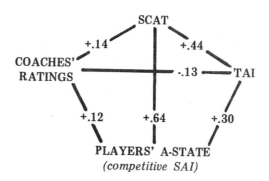

Figure 5.5. Study 8: Relationships among three measures of A-trait and players' competitive SAI scores.

As mentioned in Chapter 3, among the criteria that SCAT must meet as a measure of competitive A-trait is the capacity to predict A-states in competitive situations better than existing general A-trait inventories. From the data available in Study 8, it was possible to directly compare the predictive power of SCAT with the TAI in both competitive and noncompetitive situations. This comparison, shown in Table 19, clearly indicates the superior predictive power of SCAT in a competitive situation. The TAI, however, is a somewhat better predictor of A-states in a noncompetitive situation.

We also speculated that the relationship between SCAT and A-state would be greater for starters than for nonstarters. The starters were those five players beginning the game. In Table 19 results are presented that support this speculation. The same comparison was also made for the TAI and A-state. The difference

Table 19

Study 8: Comparison of SCAT and TAI's Ability to Predict
A-states in Competitive and Noncompetitive Situations

A-trait Scale	Situation	
	Noncompetitive	Competitive
SCAT	.25	.64
TAI	.44	.30

between starters and nonstarters in this latter case was not nearly as large as that obtained with SCAT.

Table 20

Study 8: The Prediction of A-state by SCAT
and the TAI for Starters and Nonstarters

	n	SCAT-A-state	TAI-A-state
Starters	76	.68	.35
Nonstarters	37	.49	.29

Study 9

The purpose of Study 9 was to compare SCAT and the TAI as predictors of A-states for the basketball players in the 12 situations described in Study 7. It was expected that SCAT would be a better predictor than the TAI in all competitive situations where evaluation of performance was anticipated. Furthermore, it was expected that the greater the threat arising from competitive evaluation the better SCAT would predict A-states than the TAI.

The results of this comparison are summarized in Table 21. All correlation coefficients were corrected for attenuation because predictions were being made about hypothetical situations. SCAT was a significantly better predictor than the TAI in 6 of the 12 situations, while the TAI was never a significantly better predictor of A-states. The five highest correlations for the SCAT-A-state relationship were for Situations 4, 6, 9, 10, and 12.

Table 21

Study 9: Comparison of SCAT with the TAI as Predictors of A-states in the 12 Situations in the Basketball S-R Anxiety Inventory (N = 136)

Situation	A-trait and A-state r	SCAT and A-state r	t test for difference between r's
1	.25	.18	.67
2	.47	.36	1.09
3	.35	.28	.69
4	.35	.65	3.46***
5	.44	.53	1.02
6	.35	.56	2.27*
7	.33	.31	.23
8	.33	.40	.71
9	.34	.72	4.63***
10	.27	.59	3.57***
11	.06	.22	2.69**
12	.24	.56	3.50***

Note: All correlation coefficients are significant at the .05 level, with the exception of the A-trait-A-state coefficient for Situation 11.

*p $<$.05
**p $<$.01
***p $<$.001

Each of these items describes a situation prior to competition, or as in Situation 12, a situation of considerable anticipated evaluation during the game. Situations 1 and 11 yielded the lowest correlations between SCAT and A-states because Situation 1 was not seen as threatening and Situation 11 was threatening, but not because of anticipated competitive evaluation.

Examination of the correlations for the TAI-A-state relationship indicate that Situations 2 and 5 yielded the largest r's, but as noted, neither of these correlations were significantly better than were the correlation coefficients between SCAT and A-state levels. In general, the pattern of results indicates that SCAT is clearly a better predictor than the TAI in competitive situations, and that as the time to compete nears, SCAT's ability to predict A-state improves.

Table 22

Study 9: Comparison of SCAT and the TAI as Predictors of A-states in Actual and Hypothetical Situations

Situations in Which A-states Were Measured	TAI and A-state r	SCAT and A-state r
Noncompetitive		
Actual	.44	.25
Hypothetical No. 1	.22	.16
Hypothetical No. 2	.41	.32
Precompetitive		
Actual	.30	.65
Hypothetical No. 4	.31	.57
Hypothetical No. 9	.30	.63
Hypothetical No. 10	.24	.52

Note: For comparability all correlation coefficients have been corrected for attenuation.

A final comparison of considerable significance was made between the results reported here and those obtained in Study 6. The ability of SCAT and the TAI to predict A-states in both actual and hypothetical situations was compared to determine the validity of the basketball S-R anxiety inventory. As shown in Table 22, the correlations are similar for the actual and hypothetical situations in both the noncompetitive and competitive situations. These similarities indicate that subjects' responses to psychological inventories are not unlike their responses in similar actual competitive situations.

A-Trait, A-State, and Motor Performance

At the present time, we know little about how anxiety and motor behavior are related as reviewed in Chapter 2. I suggested in "Arousal and Motor Performance" (see Appendix) that an alternative to studying the relationship between general A-trait and motor behavior is to investigate the relationship between situation-specific A-trait and motor behavior in that situation. The next two studies follow this suggestion for competitive A-trait.

Studies 10 and 11

Studies 10 and 11 are extensions of Studies 1 and 2, with the focal point being on the motor performance of the subjects rather than their A-state responses. The major hypothesis of these two studies was that high competitive A-trait subjects perform poorer than low competitive A-trait subjects in competitive situations, but no performance differences were expected between high and low competitive A-trait persons in a noncompetitive situation. This hypothesis is based on the assumption that high competitive A-trait persons manifest higher A-state levels than low competitive A-trait persons in competitive situations. Based on drive theory, higher A-states are expected to interfere with task execution during the initial stages of performance on complex motor tasks such as the motor maze task described in Studies 1 and 2.

In both Studies 10 and 11 the subjects performed 20 trials on the task. As reported in Studies 1 and 2 high competitive A-trait persons in both experiments manifested higher A-states than low competitive A-trait persons in competitive situations. The results of the effects of competitive A-trait on motor performance for these same subjects, however, indicated no significant differences between high and low SCAT persons. In order to ascertain if the A-state scores for the high and low SCAT subjects mediated the relationship between motor performance and competitive A-trait, subjects' SCAT and A-state scores were both used as predictors in a multiple regression model with the motor performance scores as the dependent variable. Two different multiple regression models were used for each experiment. The first multiple regression model determined if SCAT and A-state scores predicted motor performance using a linear equation. The second multiple regression model determined if SCAT predicted motor performance linearly and if A-state scores predicted motor performance curvilinearly. The curvilinear equation determined the predictive power of A-state scores for motor performance according to the inverted-U hypothesis. The results from each of these multiple regression analyses for both experiments indicated that neither SCAT nor A-state scores were able to significantly predict the subjects' motor performance.

What does the failure of SCAT to predict motor performance in Studies 10 and 11 mean? It does not mean that SCAT lacks construct validity. In Figure 5.6 a simple model of the relationship among A-trait, A-state, and motor performance is shown. As can be seen, competitive A-trait is theorized to predict A-state (Link 1), and then A-state is theorized to predict motor performance (Link 2). Thus, the prediction of motor performance by competitive A-trait is mediated by A-state. In the nine previous studies evidence has been presented that competitive A-trait is predictably or reliably related to A-states in competitive situations (Link 1). This evidence reflects SCAT's construct validity.

COMPETITIVE A-TRAIT	— 1 →	A-STATE	— 2 →	MOTOR PERFORMANCE

Figure 5.6. The relationship between competitive A-trait and motor performance as mediated by A-states.

The failure of SCAT and A-state to predict motor performance in Studies 10 and 11 is not negative evidence of SCAT's validity. It is evidence that a simple measure of A-state is not an adequate predictor of motor performance (Link 2). Recall that in Studies

1 and 2, which reported the relationship shown in Link 1 for Studies 10 and 11, SCAT was a significant predictor of A-state.

Predicting Motor Performance

A comment on why A-state does not predict motor performance in Studies 10 and 11 and in other research reviewed in Chapter 2 and the Appendix is in order here. Methodolotical problems, individual and task differences, and experiments of low sensitivity may all account for past failures of A-state to predict motor performance. For example, as we noted in Studies 1 and 2, the A-state levels created in laboratory experiments are not nearly as great as in field studies. This may explain why Studies 10 and 11 failed to find A-state, and hence competitive A-trait, to be significant predictors of motor performance. It also may be that a number of intervening variables need to be added to the model in Figure 5.6 to accurately discern the relationship between A-state and motor performance.

While typically it is postulated that the weak measurement of A-state is one reason for the failure to understand Link 2, I think it also needs to be recognized that we often use weak measures of motor performance. To obtain a better understanding of Link 2, we cannot just measure performance outcome (the end product of the movement), but we must measure the movement itself. A recent experiment by Weinberg (1977), illustrates this point with a study that obtained some noteworthy findings.

Weinberg selected 10 high and 10 low A-trait subjects who scored on the extremes of Spielberger's TAI. Using Spielberger's SAI, he obtained all subjects' A-state in a resting condition. Then he gave them motivating instructions for throwing a tennis ball at a target. The subjects received 10 trials and then received negative feedback about their performance, threw another 10 trials and then retook the A-state scale.

Weinberg compared the A-state scores of the low and high A-trait subjects by computing an analysis of covariance using the initial A-state scores as a covariate. The results showed that high

A-trait subjects were significantly higher in A-state after the experiment than the low A-trait subjects (see Table 23). These findings are not surprising, but the performance results were. As shown in Table 23, the performance of high A-trait subjects was compared to the performance of low A-trait subjects on the last 10 trials, using the first 10 trials as a covariate. The low A-trait subjects performed over 50% better than the high A-trait subjects.

Table 23
A-state and Performance Results Obtained by Weinberg (1976)

A-trait	A-state		Performance	
	Basal	Post-Experimental	Trials 1-10	Trials 11-20
Low	28.2	33.4	10.3	16.5
High	35.9	46.4	10.2	9.3

While this dramatic difference in performance warrants attention and replication, the unique part of Weinberg's study is that he monitored the subjects' performances through several electromyographic measures that assessed the electrical activity of the muscles involved in throwing the tennis ball. These measures of the movement itself revealed that high A-trait subjects used more energy over a longer period of time after the throw than low A-trait subjects (perseveration). In addition, high A-trait subjects exhibited co-contraction of agonists and antagonists, while low A-trait subjects exhibited sequential action. These findings were obtained both before and after the failure feedback.

Thus, while Weinberg's performance differences are probably the largest yet reported for any motor task, what makes his study unique is the clear electromyographic differences between high and low A-trait subjects. Further research using such measures of the movement process, especially in conjunction with competitive A-trait instead of general A-trait, appears promising.

In summary, this chapter has presented considerable evidence that SCAT is capable of predicting A-state prior to and during competition. The findings of Studies 10 and 11, as well as the evidence reviewed in Chapter 2 and the Appendix, indicate that knowledge of A-states alone does not provide an adequate base for predicting motor performance. Some of the reasons as to why A-state does not predict motor performance were mentioned. The important point is that the inability of SCAT to predict motor performance is not a measure of SCAT's validity. In fact, when we understand the relationship expressed by Link 2 in Figure 5.6, only then will competitive A-trait become an important predictor of motor performance. In other words, there is no theoretical reason to believe that competitive A-trait is directly related to motor performance. Competitive A-trait will predict performance only to the extent that high competitive A-trait persons differ in the degree of A-state they manifest when compared with low competitive A-trait persons.

Finally, it may be of value to mention that the prediction of motor performance is not the only dependent variable worthy of study. Predicting satisfaction from sport participation, personality development as a consequence of sport participation, and interpersonal behaviors in sport are alternative dependent variables of importance. The relationship of competitive A-trait to these variables is equally worthy of study by sport psychologists.

Other Research

At the present time several researchers have indicated they are using SCAT in their research. As their work is reported, additional evidence concerning the reliability and validity of SCAT will accumulate. Furthermore, validation of SCAT by researchers independent of the test developers is important. At present, I have received reports of two studies using SCAT.

Gerson and Deshaies (Note 6) examined the relationship between SCAT and A-state, as measured by the competitive short form of Spielberger's SAI. The subjects ($N = 107$) were female varsity intercollegiate softball players competing in the National Women's

Intercollegiate Softball Tournament. SCAT and the competitive SAI were given about 30 minutes before gametime on the second day of the tournament. The correlation between SCAT and A-state was .59 which accounts for 35% of the shared variance.

As part of a major field study, Scanlan and Passer (1976) investigated the relationship between competitive A-trait and A-state by testing 162 boys, 11-12 years old, participating in youth soccer in Los Angeles. SCAT and Spielberger's (1973) SAIC were given prior to the season. A-states were reassessed 30 minutes before the eighth game of the season and immediately after this game. SCAT was a significant predictor of the basal A-state taken prior to the season ($r = .43$, $p < .01$) and of pregame A-state ($r = .52$, $p < .01$), but not of the postgame A-state ($r = .06$). These relationships showed that boys higher in competitive A-trait had higher A-states than boys low in competitive A-trait before the season, before the 8th game, but not after the game. SCAT remained a significant predictor of pregame A-state even when basal A-state was used as a covariate, $F(1,159) = 25.61$, $p < .001$.

Additionally, Scanlan and Passer found that the winning players were lower in A-state than losing players after the game when basal A-state, pregame A-state, and SCAT were used as covariates, $F(1, 157) = 129.04$, $p < .001$. These results provide additional evidence of the construct validity of SCAT.

Summary

Substantial evidence has been presented to support the construct validity of SCAT from both experimental laboratory studies and field studies. With improved measurement of A-states (competitive short form of the SAI), SCAT was able to predict to a substantial degree the A-state levels of persons anticipating competition. Using hypothetical competitive situations, SCAT increased its ability to predict A-states as the threat in the competitive situation increased. Finally, it was found that SCAT, and SCAT along with the associated A-states, were unable to reliably predict subjects' motor performance.

CHAPTER 6

USING SCAT

The Sport Competition Anxiety Test (SCAT) is an A-trait scale designed for measuring a predisposition to respond with varying levels of A-state in competitive sport situations. SCAT was constructed primarily for research purposes to identify subjects varying in competitive A-trait. SCAT has both a child form (SCAT-C) for children ranging in age from 10 through 14 and an adult form (SCAT-A) for persons 15 years of age and older (or the reading level of the average 15 year old). The usefulness of SCAT as a diagnostic instrument for clinical purposes has not been established. Norms are available, however, for both males and females ranging in age from 10 years through college-age adults.

SCAT and the Measurement of A-state

Because SCAT is primarily a means of identifying individual differences in A-states in competitive situations, some assessment of A-states will usually be made in conjunction with SCAT. In our initial validation studies, the State Anxiety Inventory (SAI) was used because of its careful development and extensive validation, and because it is not situationally limited. As reported in Chapter 5, we have developed an abbreviated version of the adult SAI which is particularly sensitive to measuring A-states in *competitive* situations. In Chapter 7, the development of this modified scale is described and the measurement of A-states is discussed further.

Administration of SCAT

Both forms of SCAT are self-administering and may be taken either alone or in groups. The inventory has no time limits, but normally less than five minutes are required for its completion. Instruction for taking the test are printed on the inventory.

Because SCAT has considerable face validity among the ten items, five spurious statements have been added to the scale in order to diminish response bias toward the actual test items. These five items are *not* scored. The scale should be presented to subjects as the Illinois Competition Questionnaire. To alleviate the possibility of biased responding, the title and spurious items should be used.

The most important part of the instructions when administering the scale is making sure that the subject responds to each item according to how he or she *generally feels* in competitive sport situations. If the SAI or the modified competitive SAI are used in conjunction with SCAT, the respondent should be aware of how the scales differ. These A-state inventories require the respondent to report how he feels *at this moment*, not how he generally feels. For most respondents, particularly children, it is useful to have the examiner read the instructions aloud. Before beginning, make sure the instructions are completely understood. The examiner should answer questions by reiterating or clarifying the instructions. Do not offer any information regarding the purpose of the test. Be sure to instruct the respondent to answer all items.

When both an A-state scale and SCAT are used, it is recommended that the A-state scale be given first followed by SCAT. The responses to the A-state scale may be influenced by having responded to SCAT immediately before.

Scoring

The procedure for scoring SCAT is identical for both forms. For each item one of three responses are possible: (a) Hardly ever, (b) Sometimes, and (c) Often. The 10 test items are: 2, 3, 5, 6, 8, 9, 11, 12, 14, and 15. The spurious items: 1, 4, 7, 10, and 13, are *not* scored. Items 2, 3, 5, 8, 9, 12, 14, and 15 are worded so that they are scored according to the following key:

1 = Hardly ever

2 = Sometimes

3 = Often

Items 6 and 11 are scored according to the following key:

1 = Often

2 = Sometimes

3 = Hardly ever

The range of scores on SCAT is from 10 (low competitive A-trait) to 30 (high competitive A-trait).

If a person deletes 1 of the 10 test items, his prorated full-scale score can be obtained by computing the mean score for the 9 items answered, multiplying this value by 10, and rounding the product to the next whole number. When two or more items are omitted, the respondent's questionnaire should be invalidated.

For ease in hand scoring a scoring template can be made. When SCAT is used with large numbers machine-scored answer sheets may be preferable.

The Inventories

SCAT-C and SCAT-A are reproduced in Tables 24 and 25, respectively.

Norms

This section provides normative information in order to compare a person's SCAT score with appropriate reference groups. Percentile ranks and standard scores are provided for each norm group. The percentile rank of a person's score indicates the percentage of people in the norm group who scored lower on SCAT. Thus, a percentile rank of 63 indicates that 63% of the people in the norm group scored lower.

Standard scores are also provided because percentile ranks represent measurement on an ordinal scale only, while standard scores are expressed on an interval scale. A standard score is simply the deviation of a raw score from the mean expressed in standard deviation units,

$$z = \frac{x - M}{s}$$

where z = a standard score, x = a specified raw score, and M = the mean and s = the standard deviation of the raw score distribution. The z scores were transformed by setting the mean to 50 and the standard deviation to 10. Thus, the transformed z is:

$$z = 50 + 10z$$

This transformation is linear as contrasted to an area transformation which is used to obtain a normalized standard score. The normalized standard score permits reference to a standard distribution (the normal curve) and direct conversion to percentiles. If the norm group closely approximates a normal distribution, then both the unnormalized and normalized standard scores

Table 24

Sport Competition Anxiety Test for Adults

ILLINOIS COMPETITION QUESTIONNAIRE

Form A

Directions: Below are some statements about how persons feel when they compete in sports and games. Read each statement and decide if you HARDLY-EVER, or SOMETIMES, or OFTEN feel this way when you compete in sports and games. If your choice is HARDLY-EVER, blacken the square labeled A, if your choice is SOMETIMES, blacken the square labeled B, and if your choice is OFTEN, blacken the square labeled C. There are no right or wrong answers. Do not spend too much time on any one statement. *Remember* to choose the word that decribes how you *usually* feel when competing in *sports and games.*

	Hardly-Ever	Sometimes	Often
1. Competing against others is socially enjoyable.	A ☐	B ☐	C ☐
2. Before I compete I feel uneasy.	A ☐	B ☐	C ☐
3. Before I compete I worry about not performing well.	A ☐	B ☐	C ☐
4. I am a good sportsman when I compete.	A ☐	B ☐	C ☐
5. When I compete I worry about making mistakes.	A ☐	B ☐	C ☐
6. Before I compete I am calm.	A ☐	B ☐	C ☐
7. Setting a goal is important when competing.	A ☐	B ☐	C ☐
8. Before I compete I get a queasy feeling in my stomach.	A ☐	B ☐	C ☐
9. Just before competing I notice my heart beats faster than usual.	A ☐	B ☐	C ☐
10. I like to compete in games that demand considerable physical energy.	A ☐	B ☐	C ☐
11. Before I compete I feel relaxed.	A ☐	B ☐	C ☐
12. Before I compete I am nervous.	A ☐	B ☐	C ☐
13. Team sports are more exciting than individual sports.	A ☐	B ☐	C ☐
14. I get nervous wanting to start the game.	A ☐	B ☐	C ☐
15. Before I compete I usually get up tight.	A ☐	B ☐	C ☐

Table 25

Sport Competition Anxiety Test for Children

ILLINOIS COMPETITION QUESTIONNAIRE
Form C

Directions: We want to know how you feel about *competition*. You know what competition is. We all compete. We try to do better than our brother or sister or friend at something. We try to score more points in a game. We try to get the best grade in class or win a prize that we want. We all compete in sports and games. Below are some sentences about how boys and girls feel when they compete in sports and games. Read each statement below and decide if *you* HARDLY-EVER, or SOMETIMES, or OFTEN feel this way when you compete in sports and games. Mark A if your choice is HARDLY-EVER, mark B if you choose SOMETIMES, and mark C if you choose OFTEN. There are no right or wrong answers. Do not spend too much time on any one statement. *Remember* choose the word which describes how you *usually* feel when competing in *sports and games*.

	Hardly-Ever	Sometimes	Often
1. Competing against others is fun.	A ☐	B ☐	C ☐
2. Before I compete I feel uneasy.	A ☐	B ☐	C ☐
3. Before I compete I worry about not performing well.	A ☐	B ☐	C ☐
4. I am a good sportsman when I compete.	A ☐	B ☐	C ☐
5. When I compete I worry about making mistakes.	A ☐	B ☐	C ☐
6. Before I compete I am calm.	A ☐	B ☐	C ☐
7. Setting a goal is important when competing.	A ☐	B ☐	C ☐
8. Before I compete I get a funny feeling in my stomach	A ☐	B ☐	C ☐
9. Just before competing I notice my heart beats faster than usual.	A ☐	B ☐	C ☐
10. I like rough games.	A ☐	B ☐	C ☐
11. Before I compete I feel relaxed.	A ☐	B ☐	C ☐
12. Before I compete I am nervous.	A ☐	B ☐	C ☐
13. Team sports are more exciting than individual sports.	A ☐	B ☐	C ☐
14. I get nervous wanting to start the game.	A ☐	B ☐	C ☐
15. Before I compete I usually get up tight.	A ☐	B ☐	C ☐

will be the same. Both standard scores were computed, and for all norm groups the two standard scores were identical for the first two places.

The interpretation of the standard scores is based on standard deviation units. A standard score of 60 indicates a score of one standard deviation above the mean of the distribution. A score of 35 represents one and one-half standard deviations below the mean.

A summary of the test statistics for the eight norm groups is presented in Table 26. It is noteworthy that there is a trend for competitive A-trait to increase with age, slightly more so for females than males. Females on the average were higher in competitive A-trait than males for all groups. The norms for each of the eight norm groups are given in Tables 27-30.

Table 26
Summary of Test Statistics for Norm Samples

Sample	N	M	SD
4th-6th Grade (SCAT-C)			
Male	237	18.89	4.56
Female	241	19.71	4.40
7th-9th Grade (SCAT-C)			
Male	841	19.32	4.64
Female	270	20.36	5.12
10th-12th Grade (SCAT-A)			
Male	129	20.03	3.94
Female	113	22.22	4.40
College Age Adults (SCAT-A)			
Male	370	19.74	4.68
Female	158	22.60	4.87

Table 27
SCAT-C Norms for Normal Children, Grades 4-6

Raw Score	MALE		FEMALE	
	Standard Score	Percentile	Standard Score	Percentile
30	744	99	734	99
29	722	99	711	99
28	700	99	688	98
27	678	97	666	97
26	656	95	643	92
25	634	90	620	88
24	612	87	597	85
23	590	84	575	80
22	568	77	552	74
21	546	71	529	67
20	524	63	507	56
19	502	56	484	48
18	480	46	461	39
17	458	41	438	31
16	436	33	416	24
15	415	28	393	16
14	393	21	370	14
13	371	13	347	10
12	349	9	325	6
11	327	2	302	2
10	305	1	279	1

Table 28

SCAT-C Norms for Normal Children, Grades 7-9

Raw Score	MALE		FEMALE	
	Standard Score	Percentile	Standard Score	Percentile
30	730	99	688	99
29	709	99	669	97
28	687	99	649	96
27	665	97	630	91
26	644	93	610	88
25	622	90	591	84
24	601	85	571	76
23	579	79	552	70
22	558	73	532	63
21	536	66	513	53
20	515	59	493	49
19	493	51	473	42
18	472	43	454	35
17	450	37	434	30
16	429	30	415	26
15	407	24	395	19
14	386	18	376	17
13	364	12	356	12
12	342	8	337	9
11	321	4	317	5
10	299	2	298	2

Table 29
SCAT-A Norms for Normal Young Adults, Grades 10-12

| Raw Score | MALE | | FEMALE | |
	Standard Score	Percentile	Standard Score	Percentile
30	753	99	677	99
29	727	99	654	98
28	702	98	631	92
27	677	98	609	85
26	651	93	586	80
25	626	89	563	74
24	601	87	540	66
23	575	78	518	59
22	550	73	495	50
21	525	67	472	42
20	499	61	450	39
19	474	48	427	30
18	448	39	404	23
17	423	24	381	16
16	398	18	359	10
15	372	12	336	5
14	347	7	313	3
13	322	5	291	3
12	296	2	268	2
11			245	1

Table 30
SCAT-A Norms for Normal College-Age Adults

Raw Score	MALE		FEMALE	
	Standard Score	Percentile	Standard Score	Percentile
30	719	99	652	99
29	698	99	631	93
28	677	97	611	88
27	655	93	590	82
26	634	89	570	75
25	612	86	549	65
24	591	82	529	59
23	570	78	508	53
22	548	74	488	47
21	527	69	467	42
20	505	61	447	35
19	484	50	426	28
18	463	40	406	22
17	441	30	385	15
16	420	24	365	10
15	399	18	344	8
14	377	14	323	6
13	356	9	303	4
12	334	7	282	3
11	313	5	262	2
10	292	1	241	1

CHAPTER 7

MEASUREMENT OF STATE ANXIETY

Throughout this monograph, the need for a reliable and valid measure of competitive A-trait has been stressed in order to accurately predict A-states. In studying the relationship between competitive A-trait and A-state it is equally important that reliable and valid measures of A-state be made. In this chapter we briefly review the methods employed by others to assess A-state and describe the development of the competitive short form of Spielberger et al.'s (1970) A-state scale.

Physiological and Psychological Measurement of A-State

The predominant method of measuring A-state has been to use some measure of arousal. Arousal and A-state are not identical even though an arousal indicator is usually considered an appropriate method for assessing A-state. Arousal is a state of the organism varying on a continuum from deep sleep to intense excitement. It is a construct that describes the intensity of behavior but does not indicate anything about the direction of behavior. A-state was defined in Chapter 1 as negative affect — i.e., it connotes a negative direction. Thus by using arousal as a measure of A-state, it is assumed that the conditions eliciting the arousal are negative. Because the conditions normally eliciting increases in arousal in stress research are clearly seen as negative, this procedure is no problem. It is possible, however, that the use of an arousal measure as an index of A-state could reflect increases in arousal that were inferred to be negative when in fact they were positive, such as that derived from joy of curiosity. Although unlikely, researchers need to be aware of the possibility of misinterpreting the directional source of intensified behavior when the stimulus conditions eliciting arousal are ambiguous.

The measurement of arousal may be categorized into three broad classes: physiological, psychological, and behavioral. Physiological or psychophysiological measures of arousal include the measurement of brain potentials (EEG), skin resistance (GSR), cardiovascular activity (EKG), electromuscular potentials (EMG), body temperature, and biochemical changes.

A-states, while predominantly measured by physiological indicants of arousal, also have been measured by psychological inventories designed to measure arousal or to specifically measure A-states. The psychological measurement of arousal and A-states has consisted entirely of self-report inventories, asking the subject to describe his present state of activation. Thayer (1967) has described the psychological measurement of arousal as the "phenomenological awareness of general bodily functioning."

Behavioral measures of A-state or arousal have primarily consisted of measuring performance on some task and inferring different arousal states based on differences in performance. It should be clear that this assumes that the relationship between arousal and the performance measure is well understood. From the evidence reviewed in Chapter 2, it is obvious that it would be unwise to infer A-states on the basis of differences in *motor performance*. Such an interpretation, however, is often made.

Another behavioral measure of arousal that has been used is to observe such behavioral systems of heightened arousal as twitching, fidgeting, pacing, and certain body gestures. Lowe (1973), in a study of little league baseball, used such an observational system to describe the A-state of batters as they were standing in the "on deck circle" in anticipation of batting. Another recent behavioral indicator of arousal has been the use of a voice-gram which indicates the tenseness of the muscles used in speech production.

Arousal Measured Physiologically

Physiological measures of arousal are rarely found to be related to each other, to psychological measures of A-state, or to the intensity of the stressor (Lacey & Lacey, 1958). Although the intersubject correlations between physiological measures are low, it does not indicate a lack of arousal within the physiological systems following an arousing stimulus. Instead, problems arise in using any single physiological system as an indicant of arousal or in combining measurements from several systems to derive a meaningful general arousal score.

Duffy (1962) in her extensive review of the arousal literature has suggested four reasons why these correlations are low:

1. The physiological responsiveness of individuals to environmental stimuli are to some extent person-specific.
2. When the organism is activated, different physiological systems may act in compensatory fashion in order to

maintain homeostatic balance.

3. Physiological systems have different response latencies and times for reaching response limits.

4. Some physiological systems may be more representative of total organismic activation than others.

The measurement of physiological arousal also is limited because of the expensive equipment required, the limited environmental contexts in which measurements can be reliably obtained, and the difficulty in reducing massive data to a few generalizations. Levitt (1967, p. 56) concluded,

> The results, viewed as a whole, are disappointing. The four most frequently used physiological measures—blood pressure, heart rate, respiration rate, and electrical skin resistance—are components of the polygraph or lie detector, a device that enjoys an unwarranted popularity among law enforcement departments and other investigative agencies. There are really no acceptable scientific data that supports its use (Levitt, 1955).

Arousal and A-States Measured Psychologically

The psychological self-report inventory has been used frequently because of the difficulties associates with the physiological measurement of arousal. The obvious advantages of the popular self-report inventory are:

1. It can be administered and scored quickly and easily.

2. It presents no difficulties in group administration.

3. It is more reliable than physiological measures; it is less affected by extraneous factors in the environment.

Considerable difference in opinion exists about the veracity of no. 3 above. Many behavioral scientists and their fellow biological and physical scientists share the opinion that self-report data are untrustworthy. Indeed, behavioral scientists often recommend that a physiological variable be used as a concomitant measure to validate the self-report data. And the validation usually fails for the reasons mentioned in the last section. In this section, I shall attempt to explain why I believe that carefully obtained self-reports are better measures of general arousal or A-states than physiological measures, while recognizing the disadvantages of self-report data.

Thayer (1970) suggests six reasons why self-report data are mistrusted:

1. The questionnaire is based on language competence which is entirely dependent on the learning of each individual.
2. Verbal reports are voluntary responses which can be distorted at will (social desirability).
3. Private experiences that have no public observable referents are particularly dependent on the unique learning history of the individual, and therefore, potentially quite variable.
4. Depending on the form, verbal reports are influenced by response or acquiescence sets or other distorting influences.
5. A person may be unable to discriminate and label certain emotional experiences.
6. The physiological functions underlying emothional experiences may be too complex for simple verbal description.

While these are limitations, evidence indicates that a general self-report measure of arousal is a better predictor of theoretically related constructs than physiological variables. This is not at all surprising to me. When a subject is asked to respond to a self-report inventory, he must integrate all the feedback from his being, evaluate it, and describe a general arousal state. In using physiological measures, the researcher assumes that all systems are related the same way, are evaluated the same way by all subjects, and that the researcher knows how to integrate the responses from the various physiological systems. Psychophysiological research demonstrates only too well that we are unable to satisfactorily develop physiological indices of arousal that lead to reliable predictions of theoretically related constructs. Thus to ask a subject to describe his "phenomenological awareness of activation" on a self-report inventory is an extremely sensible approach at this time. Of course, this is not to imply that self-report measures of arousal are without fault; only that they have less faults than the available alternatives. Perhaps one reason that self-report data are so frequently treated with suspect is that self-reports are frequently used haphazardly. An important determinant of the reliability and validity of self-report data is the ability of the researcher to motivate the respondent to answer honestly.

Published Arousal and A-State Inventories

In this section we will describe four inventories that measure A-state. One of the first scales for measuring A-states was developed by Zuckerman (1960) and is known as the Affect Adjective Check List (AACL). The check list contains 11 anxiety-positive and 10 anxiety-negative adjectives. These items are given in Table 31. Zuckerman and Lubin (1968) reported a number of studies that together provide extensive evidence for the validity of the AACL as a measure of A-state.

Table 31
Items on the Affect Adjective Check List

Anxiety-positive	Anxiety-negative
Afraid	Calm
Desperate	Cheerful
Fearful	Contented
Frightened	Happy
Nervous	Joyful
Panicky	Loving
Shaky	Pleasant
Tense	Secure
Terrified	Steady
Upset	Thoughtful
Worrying	

The Subjective Stress Scale (SSS) was developed by Kerle and Bialek, tested and used in research by Berkun, Bialek, Kern, and Yagi (1962), and reported by Levitt (1967). The purpose of the SSS was to evaluate A-states among soldiers in simulated combat conditions. The scale is a 14 item check list in which the subject checks the one word or expression in the scale that most completely describes his strongest feeling. The scale values for the 14 items are based on research with soldiers and may not be appropriate for other populations. The items and scale values are presented in Table 32.

Table 32
Items on the Subjective Stress Scale

Item	Scale Value
Wonderful	00
Fine	09
Comfortable	17
Steady	27
Didn't bother me	40
Indifferent	48
Timid	57
Unsteady	64
Nervous	69
Worried	74
Unsafe	76
Frightened	83
Panicky	88
Scared stiff	94

Thayer (1967) developed the Activation-Deactivation Adjective Check List (AD-ACL) as an objective measure of arousal. Through factor analysis, he developed four independent activation dimensions: general activation, high activation, general deactivation, and deactivation-sleep. Thayer attempted to validate the AD-ACL by correlating it with single physiological measures and a composite of physiological measures. The results from two studies (Thayer, 1967, 1970) indicated that the correlations between single physiological measures and the AD-ACL were low, but for composite physiological measures reasonably high (.50-.60). Correlations among physiological indices were low. Thayer also developed a short-form of the AD-ACL and the items of this form are presented in Table 33. Each adjective is scored on a 4-point scale (4 = "definitely feel" and 1 = "definitely do not feel").

Table 33
Items on the Short-Form of the Activation-Deactivation Adjective Check List

General Activation	High Activation
Lively	Clutched up
Active	Jittery
Full of pep	Stirred up
Energetic	Fearful
Peppy	Intense
Vigorous	Tense
Activated	Anxious
General Deactivation	**Deactivation-Sleep**
At rest	Sleep
Still	Tired
Leisurely	Drowsy
Quiescent	Wide-awake
Quiet	Wakeful
Calm	
Placid	

Perhaps the best known inventory of A-state is the Spielberger et al. (1970) State Anxiety Inventory (SAI) which is usually used in conjunction with the Trait Anxiety Inventory (TAI). A children's form of the SAI is also available (Spielberger, 1973). The SAI has been used in much of the research reported in Chapter 5 because the psychometric qualities of this inventory and its intended function were appropriate

for our research purposes. The items that constitute the adult
form of the SAI are presented in Table 34.

Table 34
Items on the Adult Version of the State Anxiety Inventory

Items	Items
Calm	Self-confident
Secure	Nervous
Tense	Jittery
Regretful	"High strung"
At ease	Relaxed
Upset	Content
Presently worrying over possible	Worried
misfortunes	Over-excited and rattled
Rested	Joyful
Anxious	Pleasant
Comfortable	

A comparison of Tables 31-34 shows that these four inventories have considerable similarity in the items composing each
scale. The SSS and the AD-DCL were designed to measure
general activation or arousal; the AACL and SAI were constructed for the expressed purpose of measuring A-states. All
four inventories theoretically should measure A-state when
the direction of the arousing stimulus is negative. Three of
the four inventories, AACL, AD-ACL, and SAI, have impres-
sive psychometric evidence for their reliability and validity.

Competitive Short Form of the State Anxiety Inventory

As discussed in Study 5, there were two reasons for developing a short form of the SAI for competitive situations. First,
some items appeared *not* to be pertinent to measuring changes
in A-state as elicited by competitive sport situations. For
example, items such as *regretful* and *joyful* appeared to have

little relevance to anticipatory competitive A-states. Secondly, the SAI seemed long and redundant when given repeatedly. It appeared useful for repeated testing to reduce the scale by at least one-half while retaining those items more discriminating in competitive situations.

The modification process began by factor analyzing the SAI to determine if certain factors could be identified that were more sensitive to variations in A-state among persons varying in competitive A-trait. A principal component factor analysis was computed and was followed with Kaiser's varimax rotation method. The analyses were computed separately on the precompetitive A-state 1 and 2 scores in Study 4 and the precompetitive A-state scores in Study 5. Analyses of these scores were considered particularly meaningful because they should identify those A-state factors sensitive to changes in A-states as a consequence of competition. The orthogonally rotated factor weightings for the three A-state data sets are given in Tables 35-37.

The factors extracted from each of the three data sets showed little similarity to each other, particularly comparing those factors extracted from Studies 4 and 5. In some of the factors a deactivation, activation, and extreme activation commonality appeared. But, the same items were not consistently loading high for these commonalities for the different data sets.

Although the extracted factors were dissimilar for the three data sets, it was decided to use factor scores in analyzing the relationship between SCAT and A-state because the variance attributable to A-state responses could be accounted for by the five factors in each data set. The regression and correlation coefficients among SCAT and the five factor scores, as well as the student's t test for the three data sets are presented in Tables 38-40. These analyses for each data set were computed to identify which factors significantly related with SCAT and which items were more sensitive to changes in competitive situations.

Table 35
Varimax Orthogonally Rotated Factor Matrix for
Precompetitive A-state 1 Scores in Study 4

Item	Factor 1	Factor 2	Factor 3	Factor 4	Factor 5
Calm	.75*	-.14	.20	.27	.13
Secure	.66*	.23	.12	.19	.00
Tense	.41	.18	-.07	.67*	.11
Regretful	-.15	.70*	.04	-.07	.44
At Ease	.87*	-.10	-.06	.12	-.04
Upset	-.02	.36	.63*	.17	.42
Worry over misfortune	.08	.63*	-.16	.05	.09
Rested	.52*	-.13	-.23	-.40	.25
Anxious	-.17	-.05	.04	.72*	.33
Comfortable	.78*	.31	.13	-.02	.13
Self-confident	.61*	.49	.06	-.27	-.29
Nervous	.44	.41	.09	.66*	.04
Jittery	.36	.55*	.12	.47	.35
High strung	.17	.11	-.12	.20	.84*
Relaxed	.82*	-.01	.08	.11	.18
Content	.71*	.16	.25	-.06	.12
Worried	.10	.73*	.18	.29	.03
Over-excited	.19	.22	.15	.14	.72*
Joyful	.13	.01	.87*	.02	-.12
Pleasant	.25	-.12	.90*	-.01	.05
Variance	4.90	2.60	2.27	2.19	2.10
Pct. Variance	34.85	18.48	16.17	15.55	14.95
Cum. Pct. Variance	34.85	53.33	69.51	85.05	100.00

*Highest weighting for the item

Table 36

Varimax Orthogonally Rotated Factor Matrix for
Precompetitive A-state 2 Scores in Study 4

Item	Factor 1	Factor 2	Factor 3	Factor 4	Factor 5
Calm	.89*	.04	.16	.09	-.05
Secure	.81*	.20	-.02	.05	.11
Tense	.29	.07	.33	.68*	-.26
Regretful	-.26	.47	.11	.42	.58*
At Ease	.80*	.28	.30	.15	.08
Upset	-.07	.51	.19	.52	.56*
Worry over misfortune	.17	-.07	.08	.82*	.18
Rested	.07	.21	.23	.16	.71*
Anxious	.02	-.35	.53*	.21	-.45
Comfortable	.64*	.20	.15	.32	.19
Self-confident	.38	.03	-.14	-.08	.79*
Nervous	.48	.00	.64*	.40	.00
Jittery	.26	.22	.67*	.34	.14
Highstrung	.13	.00	.86*	-.03	-.05
Relaxed	.47	.57*	.02	.32	-.04
Content	.39	.71*	.01	.04	.05
Worried	.43	.04	.40	.52*	.19
Over-excited	-.01	.13	.72*	.12	.17
Joyful	.08	.76*	.14	-.13	.29
Pleasant	.17	.87*	.02	.03	.13
Variance	3.73	3.04	2.96	2.46	2.32
Pct. Variance	25.73	20.92	20.39	16.98	15.98
Cum. Pct. Variance	27.73	46.65	67.04	84.02	100.00

*Highest weighting for the item

Table 37
Varimax Orthogonally Rotated Factor Matrix for
Precompetitive A-state Scores in Study 5

Item	Factor 1	Factor 2	Factor 3	Factor 4	Factor 5
Calm	.32	.22	.15	.41*	.38
Secure	.71*	.02	.03	.06	.12
Tense	.64*	.06	-.08	.00	.32
Regretful	.71*	.11	.10	.09	-.17
At Ease	.00	.05	-.08	.84*	-.10
Upset	.44	.35	.06	.57*	.22
Worry over Misfortune	.49	.31	.13	.50*	.26
Rested	.52*	.12	.16	.40	.03
Anxious	.75*	.19	.22	.10	.01
Comfortable	.40	.21	.02	.50*	.23
Self-confident	.05	.78*	.21	.28	.01
Nervous	.29	.57*	.44	.02	-.20
Jittery	-.01	.72*	.21	.10	.27
Highstrung	.05	.06	.24	.00	.75*
Relaxed	.14	.45	.20	.13	.52*
Content	.34	.56*	-.02	-.43	.13
Worried	.22	.76*	.14	.19	.12
Over-excited	.18	.16	.73*	.21	.09
Joyful	.07	.13	.85*	-.14	.15
Pleasant	.00	.31	.75*	.00	.29
Variance	3.28	3.06	2.35	2.27	1.58
Pct. Variance	26.15	24.43	18.74	18.11	12.58
Cum. Pct. Variance	26.15	50.58	69.31	87.42	100.00

*Highest weighting for the item

Table 38

**Regression and Correlation Coefficients for SCAT and Five Factor
Scores for Precompetitive A-state 1 Scores in Study 4**

Factor	Regression Equation	r	Students t	p
1	Y = .06X - 1.14	.25	1.81	.05
2	Y = .06X - 1.19	.26	1.90	.05
3	Y = .0003X - .006	.00	.01	—
4	Y = .06X - 1.13	.24	1.79	.05
5	Y = .07X + 1.41	-.31	-2.27	.025

Table 39

**Regression and Correlation Coefficients for SCAT and
Five Factor Scores for Precompetitive A-state 2 Scores in Study 4**

Factor	Regression Equation	r	Students t	p
1	Y = .03X - .56	.12	.87	-
2	Y = .01X - .21	.05	.32	-
3	Y = .07X - 1.37	.30	2.21	.025
4	Y = .02X - .47	.10	.73	-
5	Y = .09X - 1.73	.38	2.88	.01

Table 40

**Regression and Correlation Coefficients for SCAT and
Five Factor Scores for Precompetitive A-state Scores in Study 5**

Factor	Regression Equation	r	Students t	p
1	Y = .07X - 1.42	.27	3.04	.01
2	Y = .07X - 1.51	.29	3.25	.01
3	Y = .03X - .54	.11	1.13	-
4	Y = .04X - .93	.18	1.94	.05
5	Y = .002X - 5.18	.01	.11	-

From inspection of the SAI and from the factor analyses of the three data sets, two components of A-state were subjectively extracted. These components were *activation* and *deactivation;* activation measuring high levels of A-state and deactivation measuring low levels of A-state. Three criteria were then developed for the selection of five deactivation items and five activation items which constituted the 10-item modified A-state scale. These criteria were:

1. The item had face validity for competitive sport situations
2. The item had significant weight among the orthogonally rotated factors that related significantly with SCAT for the competitive A-state scores.
3. The item had concurrent validity with Thayer's (1967) AD-ACL inventory.

Based on these criteria, the 10 items that were selected, along with the factor weightings on which the item loaded above .30, are given in Table 41. A comparison of the competitive short form of the SAI with the AD-ACL short form in Table 42 shows a marked similarity between the items in the two inventories.

Although considerably more work needs to be done to validate the competitive short form of the SAI, two additional points support its use in competitive situations. First, Spielberger points out that as few as 5 items from the SAI may be used as a subscale. Thus, the competitive short form of the SAI, because it is an abbreviated form of the SAI, has the support of the validation research completed by Spielberger et al. (1970). Secondly, of the evidence presented in Chapter 5, the competitive short form of the SAI provided the best indication of changes in A-state as a function of competition. As reported in Study 7 it appears that the competitive short form of the SAI provided a better measure of A-state in competitive situations, although it is possible that other changes in this experiment may be responsible for the high relationship between SCAT and A-state.

Table 41

Items on the Competitive Short Form of the SAI with Weightings
From Those Factors Significantly Related with SCAT

	Study 4			Study 5		
	Precompetitive A-State 1		Precompetitive A-State 2	Precompetitive A-State		
Activation Scale	Factor 4	Factor 5	Factor 3	Factor 1	Factor 2	Factor 3
Anxious	.72	.33	.53	.75	—	—
Nervous	.66	—	.64	—	.57	—
Jittery	.47	.35	.67	—	.72	—
Tense	.67	—	.33	.64	—	—
Over-excited	—	.72	.72	—	—	.73
De-Activation Scale	Factor 1	Factor	Factor 1	Factor 1	Factor 4	Factor 5
Secure	.66		.81	.71	—	—
At ease	.87		.80	—	.84	—
Comfortable	.78		.64	.40	.50	—
Calm	.75		.89	.32	.42	—
Relaxed	.82		.47	—	—	.52

Although further research will help determine the validity of the competitive short form of the SAI, its use is recommended when wishing to measure A-state in competitive sport situations. After spending several years attempting to measure arousal by a variety of physiological and psychological inventories, I am convinced that the assessment of A-state through self-report tells us more about the subject's general state of arousal than any single or composite index of physiological measures.

It is not possible to reproduce the competitive short form of the SAI here because it is only a shortened form of Spielberger's copyrighted State Anxiety Inventory. To use the scale, the title, instructions, and four-choice format of Spielberger et al.'s (1970)

116

State Anxiety Inventory is used. The items used, in the order they appeared in the scale, are presented in Table 43.

Table 42
Items on the Competitive Short Form of the SAI and Thayer's AD-ACL Short Form

Competitive SAI	Thayer's AD-ACL
Activation	*High Activation*
Anxious	Anxious
Nervous	Stirred up
Jittery	Jittery
Tense	Tense
Over-excited	Clutched up
	Fearful
	Intense
Deactivation	*General Deactivation*
Secure	Quiescent
At ease	At rest
Comfortable	Quiet
Calm	Calm
Relaxed	Placid
	Still
	Leisurely

Table 43
Items on the Competitive Short Form of the State Anxiety Inventory

1. I feel at ease	6. I feel anxious
2. I feel nervous	7. I am relaxed
3. I feel comfortable	8. I am jittery
4. I am tense	9. I feel calm
5. I feel secure	10. I feel over-excited and rattled.

AROUSAL AND MOTOR PERFORMANCE
Rainer Martens[3]

Two hypotheses have been advanced to explain the relationship between changing levels of arousal and performance, and both have received attention in the motor behavior literature. The first is known as the drive theory hypothesis and the second is the Yerkes-Dodson law or, more descriptively, the inverted-U hypothesis.

The basic prediction of drive theory for the performance of complex skills has been put forth by Spence and Spence (1966). Succintly stated drive theory predicts that

$$performance = habit \ X \ drive$$

---

[3] Abridged from an article with the same title, In J. Wilmore (Ed.), *Exercise and Sport Science Review* (Vol. 2), New York: Academic Press, 1974, pp. 155-188. Reprinted with permission from the publisher.

Habit refers to the hierarchial order or dominance of correct and incorrect responses. The theory postulates that increases in drive increase the probability of the dominant response being emitted. During the early stages of skill acquisition the dominant responses are likely to be incorrect responses, but later with practice as the skill is mastered the dominant response becomes the correct response. Thus, increases in drive, hence arousal, early in the acquisition phase impairs performance, but later in the well-learned phase, increases in arousal facilitate performance. When the dominant response is the correct response, arousal and performance have a positive linear relationship (see Figure A.1). When the dominant response is the incorrect response, drive theory predictions are not as clear. It is unlikely that arousal and performance have a negative linear relationship. If performance is already of a poor quality, heightened arousal may not impair performance further. It is possible, however, that increases in arousal may suppress the rate of acquisition of the skill.

The inverted-U hypothesis, on the other hand, postulates a nonmonotonic or curvilinear relationship between arousal and performance. Also illustrated in Figure A.1, the inverted-U hypothesis predicts that performance improves with increasing levels of arousal to some optimum point, whereupon further increases in arousal cause performance impairment. As can be seen from Figure A.1, the two hypotheses make quite different predictions about the level at which maximum performance occurs. The experimental evidence testing these hypotheses for motor behavior is reviewed in the following.

Drive Theory Hypothesis and Motor Performance

The typical experimental paradign for testing the drive theory hypothesis has been to vary drive level experimentally in one of several ways so that one group of subjects is in a high drive condition and another group in a low drive condition, with other groups sometimes falling between these extremes. Then the performance differences between the groups are examined. Drive has been experimentally manipulated by exposing the subject to varying intensities of a noxious stimulation (usually called a *stressor*, or by depriving him of some need, or by identifying individuals who differ in *emotional responsiveness*. The latter procedure, sometimes in conjunction with a stressor, has been equated with drive (Spence & Spence, 1966) and has commonly been assessed by trait anxiety scales such as the Manifest Anxiety Scale (MAS). Thus, to the extent that drive is synonymous with arousal, one body of evidence examining the relationship between arousal and motor performance comes from the anxiety literature.

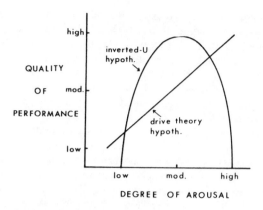

Figure A.1. The drive theory and inverted-U hypothesis of the arousal-performance relationship.

Anxiety as Drive

The majority of experimental evidence for testing the drive theory hypothesis has been reviewed elsewhere by the author (Martens, 1971, 1972). In this review twenty-eight tests of the drive theory hypothesis were made by comparing high and low drive groups as assessed by the MAS in the absence of an external stressor on a variety of motor tasks. The typical experimental paradigm used in these studies is illustrated in the study by Farber and Spence (1953). Based on scores obtained on the MAS, 40 high anxious and 40 low anxious college undergraduates performed a stylus maze task with 10 T choice points. As was hypothesized, the maze performance of the high anxious subjects was reliably poorer than that of the low anxious subjects, with the more difficult choice points providing the greatest difference between the two groups. Although twelve additional tests of the drive theory hypothesis supported the findings of Farber and Spence, fifteen tests did not support the hypothesis. Attempts to explain these equivocal findings through differences in factors such as the stage of practice or task characteristics (e.g., task difficulty or speed versus accuracy tasks) were unsuccessful.

A major assumption underlies the use of trait anxiety scales as a method of varying arousal in order to test the arousal-motor performance relationship. These scales assume a chronic view of anxiety, i.e., individuals high in trait anxiety are considered to be in a constantly higher arousal state than are low trait anxiety individuals. The general consensus among anxiety researchers today, however, is in opposition to this position (Spielberger, 1966b), and even Spence and Spence (1966) shy away from this assumption.

Instead, trait anxiety is viewed as a personality trait that predisposes a person to manifest higher levels of arousal only when confronted with stressful situations. The high trait anxiety person simply perceives more situations as threatening and/or responds with greater levels of arousal than low trait anxiety persons when in these situations. The person does not show consistently higher levels of arousal at all times and to all situations. In anxiety terminology, the arousal actually manifested by a stressful or threatening situation is called *state anxiety*.

Considerable support for the trait-state distinction or the situational view of anxiety has been put forth by Spielberger (1966a; Spielberger *et al.*, 1970). Thus, if trait anxiety is simply a disposition which is only manifested by certain situational stressors, differences in performance in the absence of such situational stressors should not be expected. This may explain the fifteen tests in which no differences were found between high and low trait anxiety groups, i.e., in the absence of a stressor no changes in arousal levels existed between the two groups and, hence, no changes in performance. If this explanation is valid, it creates the perplexing situation of being unable to explain the thirteen findings supporting the drive theory hypothesis in the absence of a stressor. As yet an explanation to account adequately for these two sets of equivocal results has not been proposed.

Perhaps, then, the literature in which the drive theory hypothesis was tested by varying trait anxiety and manipulating state anxiety through the introduction of a stressor is less ambiguous. Carron and Morford (1968), for example, tested the effects of an electric shock stressor on high and low anxious subjects as determined by the MAS. Each anxiety group was divided into three subgroups: a control, an early stress group, and a late stress group. An electric shock was administered early or late in practice to the two experimental groups as they practiced on a stabilometer for seventy trials. The results failed to show reliable differences between the two anxiety groups, the presence or absence of shock, nor the interaction between the stress and anxiety. Unfortunately, for some twenty tests of the drive theory hypothesis reviewed by the author (Martens, 1971, 1972) in which a stressor was introduced, no clear support for the situational position of the drive theory hypothesis was found.

Wide variation in experimental procedures, motor tasks, and stressors made it impossible to identify any trends in the studies. The major methodological limitations of these studies has been the failure to verify by subjective reports or physiological indicants the successful change of arousal states through the introduction of a stressor. In the absence of corroborative evidence as to the effectiveness of the stressor when negative findings are obtained, it is impossible to determine whether performance was unaffected by changes in arousal or whether arousal was not effectively changed.

The use of other anxiety scales, namely the IPAT anxiety scales (Cattell, 1957; Scheier and Cattell, 1960), have been no more productive of information than the MAS. In addition, the IPAT anxiety scales have insufficient content and construct validity as measures of trait anxiety (Martens, 1972).

Thus, in summary, the use of trait anxiety scales in the absence or presence of a stressor has not shown any consistent relationship with motor performance. Unfortunately, these equivocal findings tell us little about the arousal-motor performance relationship since it is highly dubious whether changes in arousal level were effected in these studies.

In addition, a serious problem incapacitates drive theory research when extended to motor behavior. At the present time no one has been able to determine clearly the habit hierarchies for the motor responses on various motor tasks. If it is impossible to predict clearly whether the correct or incorrect response is dominant, then it is impossible to test the equation: performance = habit X drive and its derivatives. Thus, as an alternative, subjective decisions as to the habit strength of the correct and incorrect response must be made. Commonly it is assumed that when the skill is being acquired and the learning curve has not reached an asymptote, the incorrect response is dominant. After the learning curve reaches an asymptote, the correct response is assumed dominant. Because this assumption is crude at best and because of wide individual and group variation in the development of habit hierarchies, drive theory remains operationally nonfunctional for complex motor behavior.

Inverted-U Hypothesis and Motor Performance

The inverted-U hypothesis has generated enthusiastic support in the motor behavior area for several reasons. First, considerable experimental evidence has been inferred to support this hypothesis. Second, the inverted-U hypothesis has a great deal of appeal at an intuitive level. And third, an alternative hypothesis is needed because the drive theory hypothesis has not explained adequately the relationship between arousal and motor performance. In fact, the inverted-U relationship between arousal and performance has been obtained frequently enough by drive theorists that they have attempted to explain this nonmonotonic relationship through derivations of drive theory (Broen & Storms, 1961; Spence & Spence, 1966).

Yerkes and Dodson (1908) were the first to show experimental support for the inverted-U hypothesis using mice as subjects. Over the next 60 years considerable evidence accumulated in support of the inverted-U hypothesis. The experimental literature testing this hypothesis for motor behavior specifically is reviewed in the following paragraphs. For general literature reviews of the inverted-U hypothesis, the reader is referred to Courts (1942),

Broadhurst (1959), Duffy (1962), Lazarus, Deese, and Osler (1952), Malmo (1959), Levitt (1967), and Spence and Spence (1966).

Much of the evidence offered in support of the inverted-U hypothesis comes from the trait anxiety literature testing the drive theory hypothesis. Most of these studies, however, have only indirectly tested the inverted-U relationship. Instead of creating at least three distinct points on the arousal continuum, these studies compared the performance of low and high trait anxiety groups under only two levels of stress, assuming that at least three distinct points were created. That is, the low trait anxiety-low stress group was considered least aroused, the high trait anxiety-high stress group most aroused, and the low trait anxiety-high stress group and the high trait anxiety-low stress group considered to be at an intermediate level on the arousal continuum. If the low anxiety-low stress group and the high anxiety-high stress group were inferior to the other groups, the inverted-U hypothesis was proposed. However, Spence and Spence (1966) have pointed out that this is only one of several possible explanations to account for the results. In this chapter only the direct evidence testing the inverted-U hypothesis is reviewed in detail.

Several studies have tested the inverted-U hypothesis by varying three or more levels of trait anxiety. Studies by Matarazzo, Ulett, and Saslow (1955) and by Singh (1968), using a motor maze and a mirror tracing task, respectively, found that moderate trait anxiety subjects performed superior to low and high trait anxiety subjects. Matarazzo and Matarazzo (1956) and Harrington (1965), however, were unable to replicate these findings, obtaining no differences between various levels of trait anxiety using a pursuit rotor and balancing task, respectively.

These equivocal findings may result because trait anxiety does not reflect changes in arousal levels, as discussed earlier, but instead shows a disposition to respond with greater arousal to certain stimuli. Thus, a more appropriate test of the inverted-U hypothesis would be to expose high, moderate, and low trait anxiety subjects to high, moderate, and low levels of stress. Martens and Landers (1970) executed such a study with junior high school boys performing a motor tracking task. Physiological (heart rate and palmar sweating) and questionnaire data confirmed the establishment of three levels of arousal. The performance results supported the inverted-U hypothesis separately for trait anxiety and the three levels of stress. That is, the moderate trait anxiety group performed significantly better than the low and high trait anxiety groups, regardless of the stress condition, Likewise, the moderately stressed subjects performed significantly better than the nonstressed or high stressed subjects, independent of the differences in trait anxiety. These separate inverted-U's for the three stress conditions and the three trait anxiety conditions are perplexing findings, particularly when it was expected that high trait anxiety subjects would respond with greater arousal to high stress conditions than low trait anxiety subjects. In addition, the physiological and questionnaire data present a confusing picture. Although these data supported the creation of three distinct levels of arousal for the three stress conditions, the physiological data indicated no differences among the three levels of trait anxiety, yet both the trait anxiety factor and the stress factor yielded inverted-U's. The idiosyncrasies of this study remain to be explained.

Before elaborating further on the inverted-U hypothesis, several difficulties in testing this hypothesis warrant mention. A major problem has been the relatively weak experimental manipulation of arousal and the associated failure to provide corroborative physiological and/or other data to verify that changes in arousal have been created. It is very questionable whether either very low or very high arousal levels are achieved in laboratory situations. Stress researchers have also found this to be a problem, but for a solution they have turned to field studies and field experiments in order to obtain greater "impact" from environmental stimuli. Several very stressful situations have come under the scrutiny of behavioral scientists in field studies, and these studies provide us with our best data in terms of external validity regarding the arousal-performance relationship. Fortunately, several field studies pertain to motor behavior.

In two fascinating field experiments with sport parachutists (Fenz & Epstein, 1967; Fenz & Jones, 1972), it was found that the arousal level, as measured by heart rate and respiration rate, showed consistent patterns among jumpers, depending on whether they were novices or experienced jumpers and on whether they made good or poor jumps. All jumpers showed a steady increase in arousal as the time-to-jump neared, but several minutes before the actual jump the experienced jumpers began to reduce their heart rate and respiration rate to a more moderate level. Of course, the experienced jumpers made superior jumps when compared to the novices. More importantly both novice and experienced jumpers recorded this same reduction in arousal when they executed a technically "good" jump. However, when the jump was rated poor, the arousal level had not been reduced to the moderate level immediately before the jump but had remained quite high. It is important to note that the lowering of arousal occurred several minutes before the actual jump. For example, among good jumpers heart rate reached a peak of 100 beats/min at the time of "engine warmup" and declined steadily thereafter until the "jump run" at which time heart rate was 85. These very powerful and reliable findings provide strong support for the notion that moderate levels of arousal are more conducive for superior sport parachuting than extremely high levels.

Another intriguing field study by Lowe (1973) was done in a Little League baseball setting. This study compared the hitting performance of an entire league of batters over a season with the criticalness of each game in relationship to the other games and with the criticalness of the situation within any one game. For example, the criticalness of the game increased when the two teams playing one another were closer to each other in the league standings and nearer first place and the number of games remaining to be played was small. Situation criticality increased as the game progressed, the score was close, more outs were made, and more men were on base. These two criticality scores constituted the operational measure of arousal. Physiological (heart rate and respiration rate) and observational records were obtained which corroborated the operational definition of arousal.

Lowe's results showed support for the inverted-U hypothesis. Little Leaguers hit best at moderate levels of arousal than at low or high levels. Lowe postulated, however, that the task became more difficult with increasing levels of arousal. This was explained in that the better pitchers were used in the more critical games and that they threw harder in the more critical situations. Lowe then computed a task difficulty index based on the pitcher's performance and reanalyzed the hitter's performance adjusting for this difficulty factor. This index, however, seems questionable since it is equally likely that the heightened arousal may also impair the pitcher's performance. From the reanalysis, Lowe concluded that the inverted-U relationship was an artifact that was obtained only when task difficulty and arousal were varied simultaneously. Lowe suggested that the true relationship between arousal and performance is positive linear.

Lowe's study was replicated with Big Ten basketball teams for the 1969 season looking at game and situation criticality as they influenced freethrow shooting (Giambrone, 1973). Freethrow shooting had the advantage of maintaining a constant difficulty level. Both interplayer and intraplayer analyses failed to show any relationship between arousal as operationally defined by game and situation criticality and freethrow shooting. A number of factors to explain the discrepancy between these two studies was suggested by Giambrone, but no clear reason could be identified.

Perhaps, the most distressing problem in testing the inverted-U hypothesis is the inability to measure precisely points along the arousal continuum. As a consequence it is virtually impossible to know whether arousal is manipulated to its extremes, or at least on both sides of the inflection point of the inverted U-shaped performance curve. Thus, when testing the inverted-U hypothesis, if the quality of performance increases with an increase in arousal, then the preceding level of arousal is simply considered too low. If a further increase in arousal fails to result in a performance decrement, it simply is conjectured that the arousal was of insufficient intensity and higher levels are again proposed. Thus, the inverted-U hypothesis can only be supported, but, because it is impossible to know the extremes for the arousal dimension, it cannot be refuted.

In one sense, then, the inverted-U relationship is more of a *post hoc* explanation than a hypothesis. Consequently, a more fruitful strategy at this point may be not to view the inverted-U hypothesis as being correct or incorrect but instead to regard it as an issue of specifying the parameters for *when* it is correct.

Factors Mediating the Arousal-Motor Performance Relationship

Task Characteristics

Among the more obvious factors that qualify the arousal-motor performance relationship is the task. Fiske and Maddi (1961) suggest that there probably is a range of arousal levels in which maximum performance can occur and that this range varies with the dimensions of the task. At least two dimensions of the task appear to be important in determining the optimal arousal level for maximal performance: *(a)* the amount of energy that must be expended to undertake the task and *(b)* task difficulty.

Tasks obviously vary in the degree of physiological energy required to engage in the activity. Normally, we would consider the following activities to require increasing levels of physical energy, and hence, arousal, for normal participation: sleeping, reading, playing chess, throwing horseshoes, and engaging in a wrestling match. This dimension has been of little interest to psychologists, but has received considerable attention in the exercise physiology literature. The difficulty of the task within the range of physical energy demands probably determines the total arousal level demanded for maximal performance. Fiske and Maddi have postulated that the more difficult the task the narrower the range of optimal arousal for maximal performance. This postulate is shown diagramatically in Figure A.2. It may be further postulated that greater physical energy requirements combined with increasing task difficulty reduce the range of optimal arousal even further. High-energy requirements with high task difficulty are the precise task conditions that exist in many well-known sports such as tennis, basketball, and wrestling. Thus, because these activities have such a narrow range for optimal performance, it is easy to understand why it is so difficult to achieve and maintain an optimal arousal level when performing these tasks.

Individual Differences

Another set of important factors, which have been commonly thought to influence the arousal-performance relationship, are individual differences among persons. Duffy (1962) suggests that if high levels of arousal do indeed create perceptual, cognitive, or motor disorganization, the ability to

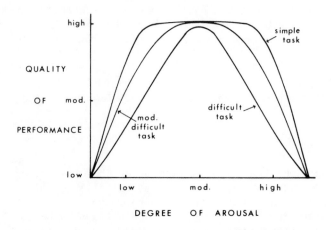

Figure A.2. Arousal-task difficulty relationship hypothesized by Fiske and Maddi (1961).

inhibit or to learn to control the organism's response to arousal-eliciting stimuli would influence the quality of performance. The personality disposition of trait anxiety is an important factor determining the responsiveness of a person to arousal-eliciting stimuli and, thus, possibly a person's inhibitory ability. As reviewed earlier, the results with general trait anxiety scales have been equivocal. It has been suggested that rather than anxiety being a unitary general construct, better understanding of anxiety would be obtained by looking at specific types of anxiety such as audience, test, and competition anxiety. There is evidence to support such a suggestion (Sarason *et al.*, 1960). Consequently, future research may show that the arousal-performance relationship is mediated only by specific stress-evoking stimuli to which the person is responsive and that these must be present in the performance situation.

Why the Inverted-U?

From the limited experimental evidence testing the relationship between arousal and motor performance, the inverted-U hypothesis appears to be favored. This conclusion was reached for the following reasons. First, the drive theory hypothesis that performance = habit X drive is not testable for motor behavior because of the inability to specify habit hierarchies for motor responses. Disregarding habit, and examining the prediction of a positive linear relationship between drive (hence arousal) and performance, the evidence is equivocal. In some cases a positive linear relationship between arousal and performance has been found, in other cases, a negative linear relationship, and in other cases, no relationship. Furthermore, not infrequently has the inverted-U relationship been obtained when testing the drive theory hypothesis. This has occurred with enough regularity that drive theorists have attempted to modify Hullian notions to explain the curvilinear relationship between arousal and performance. Finally, because of the nature of the two hypotheses, the inverted-U hypothesis tends to supersede the drive theory hypothesis. That is a positive linear relationship between arousal and performance may occur initially within the inverted-U hypothesis, but, with continued increases in arousal, performance decrement eventually occurs. Thus, with imprecise measurement of arousal levels, for those studies in which a positive linear relationship has been obtained, it is easy to conclude that arousal was not of sufficient intensity to produce impairment, particularly since, in most of these studies, what appear to be highly arousing situations have not been used. Therefore, because evidence has shown that an inverted-U relationship does occur for motor behavior under certain conditions, there is a strong tendency to conclude that this relationship exists for all complex motor responses under the "right" conditions. At least this appears to be a more parsimonious approach at this time since it does not negate the possibility of revealing a positive linear relationship under certain circumstances. The researcher's task then is to learn what these "right" conditions are.

Although experientially and experimentally we have some knowledge about the inverted-U relationship between arousal and performance, we still remain largely in the dark. We know little about what aspects of performance are affected by various levels of arousal; we are naive about the influence of diverse sources of arousal on various motor tasks; and, we have little understanding of the role of individual differences. But, most importantly, we do not know why the inverted-U relationship exists.

The previous reading was written for *Exercise and Sport Science Review.* Much of what pertained to anxiety was derived from a review article I wrote in 1971 published in the *Journal of Motor Behavior.* The same journal also published four reactions or comments about the review. Two of these reactions are presented next. Janet Taylor Spence, who developed the Manifest Anxiety Scale and with her husband pioneered research in drive theory, reacted to the review by disagreeing with two of my major conclusions. The substance of her comments are contained in the next abridged article.

APPENDIX

WHAT CAN YOU SAY ABOUT A TWENTY-YEAR OLD THEORY THAT WON'T DIE?

Janet Taylor Spence[4]

Professor Martens would obviously prefer that "drive theory" or, one suspects, almost anything associated with the Manifest Anxiety Scale (MAS), had never come into being as far as the field of motor behavior is concerned. He judges the theory to be of little predictive utility in this area and he may well be correct. He too recognizes, however, that the best hope for getting rid of an inappropriate theory is to develop a more satisfactory alternative. It is beyond my field of competence to suggest what form the latter might take as applied to motor behavior or even to evaluate meaningfully

---

[4] Abridged from an article with the same title, *Journal of Motor Behavior*, 1971, 3, no. 2, 193-203. Reprinted with permission from the author and publisher.

the methodological adequacy of the group of motor behavior studies which have borrowed some of our ideas about drive and the MAS.

. . .those of us who were involved in the development of "drive theory" have confined ourselves largely to classical conditioning and certain kinds of verbal learning, and have done little thinking about motor behavior. It now becomes appropriate to inquire what kinds of theoretical models of the latter have been used by those borrowing some of our assumptions about drive and anxiety to predict the performance of MAS groups, and how much empirical support, independent of any assumptions about anxiety, these models have. I am not sufficiently familiar with the motor behavior literature to attempt to answer these questions and have to rely on Martens for enlightenment. What Martens apparently proposed as a model was that " . . . while the skill was being acquired and the learning curve had not reached an asymptote the incorrect response was dominant. After the learning curve had become asymptotic and acquisition was indicated, the correct response was assumed to be dominant (p. 158)." It is these criteria which he used to make predictions about high and low MAS groups for each study and therefore whether or not "drive theory" was confirmed by the results. With respect to the kinds of learning situations with which I am familiar, both propositions seem to be highly dubious. At the beginning of training, incorrect response may or may not be evoked, and the correct response may be stronger or weaker than any initial competing tendencies; this depends on the task. Assuming that strong competing tendencies were initially present, the correct response may or may not be sufficiently dominant when performance reaches an asymptotic level to be immune from interfering tendencies, again depending on the task. I am not in a position to suggest, however, that the Martens analysis is an inappropriate one for motor behavior. But I should call attention to the fact that a successful "test" of drive theory depends not merely on the adequacy of our assumptions concerning the relationship between the MAS, drive, and performance, but also on the adequacy of the theoretical analysis of the task, independent of the drive factor. In the case of the Martens review, the burden of proof for the latter rests on him or others who have chosen to extend our ideas to motor behavior.

Martens too recognized the possibility that appropriate analyses may not have been made, questioning on several occasions whether it is possible to specify the habit hierarchies of motor tasks. Thus it seems reasonable to conclude, not that "drive theory" has been tried and found wanting, but with Martens that, "Hypotheses from drive theory [explaining] the functional relationship between anxiety and motor behavior cannot be tested satisfactorily until the habit hierarchy of an individual's responses can be determined (p. 172." Going even further, perhaps it is not yet even clear whether this S-R type of analysis has much utility for understanding motor behavior and therefore whether any of our notions about anxiety, drive, and performance have applicability. The same conclusion would seem to apply to any theory of anxiety and performance, such as Esterbrook's, which also depends on the availability of an appropriate theoretical model of motor behavior.

I must enter a strong demurrer, however, with Martens' contention that "the results using the MAS have failed to reveal any consistent findings (p. 172)" or that, primarily because of this, "the time has come to abandon the MAS (p. 172)," apparently in favor of some "better" measure of trait anxiety. (I am not entirely out of sympathy with his latter suggestion, but not for the reasons given.)

A reputed custom of the early Greeks was to kill the messenger who bore bad news; the suggestion that the MAS be abandoned because studies utilizing it have failed to produce results yielding simple empirical generalizations seems to be in this scapegoat mode. If there is one contribution that our studies with the MAS have made, it is to demonstrate that no simple empirical statement can be made about the relationship between anxiety and performance. This fact should not be too surprising since psychological relationships are frequently complex, and in the case of certain kinds of learning tasks, our theory has had some success in identifying the variables that must be taken into account if predictions are to be made. One sees from the tables that Martens presents that, overall, the MAS is frequently a variable contributing to performance since significant differences between groups were obtained far more often in this collection of studies than would be expected by chance. Their seeming inconsistency, however, reflects more our current inability to identify the relevant variables in motor tasks which join with the MAS in determining performance than some instability or other flaw in the MAS. The MAS does not, after all, totally lack the virtues Martens mentions—test-retest reliability, internal consistency, concurrent and construct validity, etc. More crucial, the MAS is quite strongly correlated with other trait measures. As comforting as it would be to believe that a new and better measure of general anxiety would solve most of our problems, it is thus unlikely that any currently available scale will bring about any radical improvement. What is most critical to obtain is not better anxiety scales but better theories.

The validity of general trait concepts has come under attack in recent years, some investigators suggesting the greater utility of postulating more specific predispositions which describe the particular situations in which S will exhibit particular behaviors. Whether one concludes that we should or should not continue to investigate the empirical relationship between performance and the MAS or any other general anxiety measure depends in large part on how persuasive one finds these arguments.

If one accepts that general trait concepts are useful, then the best reason I can think of for continuing to use general anxiety measures is simply that one is interested in anxious people and how they behave. But it is possible to have other kinds of interests, which require on purely empirical grounds other types of measures. Many investigators, for example, are concerned exclusively with how behavior is affected by emotional states such as anxiety, once aroused. In these instances, 2 types of approaches are feasible, sometimes in conjunction with each other. In the first, stimulus conditions said to determine emotional state are manipulated experimentally and performance under the various conditions compared. Or one may infer intensity of emotional state for each S in a given condition by obtaining some type of relevant physiological or self-report measure and correlating this response index with another concurrently measured, performance variable.

The latter type of response-inferred measure is, of course, an index of variability among individual Ss which reflects the operation of both transient, temporary factors and a collection of more stable predispositions or traits. For this reason, those who are interested in anxiety as a trait concept are well advised not to rely on these *in situ* measures but to administer, outside the experimental setting, a trait measure such as a general anxiety scale, or, as Martens recommends, a test which is more specifically oriented towards the situation one wishes to investigate: anxiety about school examinations, contact sports, swimming, interpersonal relations, etc. A number of such tests have been developed, including the all-purpose Fear Survey Schedule devised to help behavior therapists identify the specific objects or events which arouse an individual's anxieties.

Selecting Ss by means of such specific measures does not, of course, put us one iota ahead in understanding the relationship between anxiety and behavior. But this approach has an obvious advantage over the use of a general measure like the MAS in that the individual who confesses in advance that he is fearful about a particular kind of situation is more likely to exhibit anxiety when actually placed in that setting than an individual who has admitted only that he is frequently anxious but not where or when.

For investigators whose primary focus of interest is on a particular type of setting or activity and whose concern is with Ss who are characteristically fearful about it, the most sensible kind of measure to use is obviously the situationally-oriented test. Those who restrict their investigations to one particular situation and to Ss who become anxious in it also have the advantage of being able to determine relatively easily some of the major empirical facts about that situation, and can do so without any guiding theory. But there is a price to pay for this type of approach. Ss who are anxious about one object or event are undoubtedly uniquely different in many aspects of their history and current behavior, at least with respect to this particular fear, than Ss anxious about another object or event. Anxiety reactions aside, the empirical relationships between performance and the stimulus variables contributing to it are similarly not identical from one type of situation to another and even within a given class of situations, many relationships are likely to be closely tied to a particular set of external situations. To avoid the challenge of having to compile an encyclopedic handbook of the findings for every conceivable variation of every conceivable type of situation in which we might be interested—a task which would be not only monumentally time-consuming but would also yield a limited amount of information on which to base innovative procedures for behavior change—scientists have always sought empirical and theoretical principles which have some degree of generality. This was the promise that "drive theory" and its associated theoretical developments held. Unlike Erich Segal's heroine, it is no longer young, not quite as attractive as it once was, and as long as psychologists remain intrigued by the concept of anxiety, quite unlikely to die without a replacement.

Obviously, Spence (1971) has a warm spot in her heart for drive theory and the MAS, as she should after devoting 20 years of research to them. Spence said nothing, however, in her 1971 commentary that changes my opinion about the utility of drive theory or the MAS *as a measure of drive*. In my 1974 review "Arousal and Motor Performance", I restated my position and briefly commented on Spence's comments.

When drive theory has been extended to tasks other than simple conditioning and verbal learning tasks, such as motor tasks, failure to obtain support for the theory has usually led experimenters to question the validity of the MAS and/or the drive theory hypothesis. The "defenders" of drive theory, however, hasten to point out that the theory was not properly tested because the task was inappropriate (Spence, 1971), and thus, the theory and the MAS remain viable. Among the criteria for a good theory is that it is testable. The limited task parameters to which drive theory appears appropriate negates its usefulness for motor behavior.

Consequently, because of methodological deficiencies in the experimental research available and the inability to specify habit hierarchies for motor responses, the experimental evidence has not provided any insight into the arousal-motor performance relationship. Previously I criticized both the MAS and drive theory separately as they applied to motor behavior (Martens, 1971). Spence (1971) appropriately responded by suggesting that I was "throwing out the baby with the bath water." This may be true for the MAS. However, the fact still remains that drive theory itself has not led us to any clearer understanding of motor behavior.

Spence (1971) argues that the theory was not appropriately tested either because of poor research procedures or the use of inappropriate tasks. Unfortunately, all motor tasks of any interest are inappropriate. My point is that drive theory *cannot* be appropriately tested for motor behavior because of its rigorous and limited task specifications.

This view of drive theory is by no means unpopular. Particularly then for motor behavior, concurrence is given to Cofer and Appley's (1964) statement that the drive concept is not only "without utility" but actually is "a liability" in that it prevents investigators from arriving at new formulations. Moreover, this review supports Bolles' (1967) conclusion that "the worst failure of the drive concept continued to be that it does not help us to explain behavior" (p.329). [pp. 173-174]

In another reaction to my review article, Charles Spielberger clarifies the relationship between drive theory and his own trait-state conception of anxiety. In this informative article, Spielberger specifies what he believes must happen before an adequate understanding of the anxiety-motor behavior relationship can be obtained.

APPENDIX

TRAIT-STATE ANXIETY AND MOTOR BEHAVIOR

Charles D. Spielberger[5]

It is obviously not possible within the scope of the present brief paper to address the many complex theoretical and methodological questions that have been raised by Martens (1971), Carron (1971), and Marteniuk (1971). I shall try, however, to clarify several important sources of confusion with regard to the relationship between anxiety theory and drive theory, and then touch upon the significance of task complexity and individual differences in ability as these variables may influence the effects of anxiety on motor behavior.

Drive Theory proper begins with 2 assumptions: (a) Noxious or aversive stimuli arouse a hypothetical emotional response, r_e; and (b) Drive level (D) is a function of the strength of r_e. The MAS was developed as an operational measure of r_e,

---

[5] Abridged from an article with the same title, *Journal of Motor Behavior*, 1971, no. 3, 265-279. Reproduced with permission by the author and publisher.

and it was assumed that scores on this scale reflect consistent individual differences in D. Evidence of the construct validity of the MAS as an index of D has been consistently demonstrated in classical conditioning experiments in which the UCS is typically a noxious stimulus (Spence, 1964). But verbal and motor learning tasks generally do not involve noxious stimulation, and the evidence bearing on whether Ss with high anxiety, as measured by the MAS, have higher D than low anxiety Ss when performing on such tasks is inconclusive. This led Spence (1958) to propose 2 alternative hypotheses concerning the relation between MAS scores and D: (a) The "Chronic Hypothesis" posits that Ss with high MAS scores are more emotional than Ss with low scores, and are therefore higher in D in *all* situations, whether stressful or not; (b) The "Reactive Hypothesis" posits that high MAS Ss are more emotionally reactive than low MAS Ss, and respond with higher D only in situations involving some form of stress.

Investigations of anxiety and learning under neutral and stressful experimental conditions provide strong empirical support for the Reactive Hypothesis (e.g., Nicholson, 1958; Sarason, 1960; Spence & Spence, 1966; Spielberger, 1966b). Differences in the performance of Ss who differ in anxiety as measured by scales such as the MAS are obtained only when either the task or the experimental conditions involve some element of stress. For example, Spielberger and Smith (1966) found no relationship between anxiety and performance on a verbal learning task when it was given with neutral instructions, but when the same task was given with stressful instructions, anxiety impaired performance on early learning trials and facilitated performance on later trials. Apparently, the neutral instructions failed to evoke differential levels of A-state in Ss who differed in A-Trait.

While drive theory does not explicitly differentiate between trait and state anxiety, this distinction is implicit in Spence's Reactive Hypothesis which may be restated as follows: Ss high in A-Trait will respond with greater elevations in A-State than low A-Trait Ss in situations involving some form of stress. It follows that the concept of D is logically more closely associated with A-State than with A-Trait, and that the assumption that Ss with high scores on A-Trait measures will be higher in D than Ss with low A-Trait scores is questionable. It should also be apparent that drive theory must be augmented by a trait-state theory of anxiety which specifies the conditions under which Ss differing in A-Trait will be expected to show differences in A-State (D).

A critical evaluation of the research literature suggests that high A-Trait Ss tend to show performance changes attributable to higher D in situations characterized by psychological stress, such as failure or threats to self-esteem (ego-threats), but not in situations involving physical dangers or threats of harm (Spence & Spence, 1966; Spielberger, 1966a, 1972a). Thus, in order for an experimental situation to evoke differential levels of A-State in Ss who differ in A-Trait, some type of psychological stress (ego-threat) appears to be required. The extent to which drive theory has been supported in the research literature is probably due to the fact that in studies in which *Ss* were selected on the basis of extreme scores on A-Trait measures, *Ss* were also exposed to some threat to self-esteem. Conversely, we may speculate that drive theory was not supported in a number of studies because the situation was not stressful or the stressor was a physical danger rather than an ego threat.

Assuming that elevations in A-State reflect drive level, drive theory delineates the complex effects of differences in A-State (D) on performance. According to the theory, the effects of A-State on performance in a learning task will depend upon the relative strengths of the correct habits (responses) and the competing error tendencies evoked by the task. On simple tasks, in which correct responses are stronger than error tendencies, high A-State would be expected to facilitate performance. On complex or difficult tasks, in which error tendencies are stronger than correct responses, it would be anticipated that high A-State would interfere with performance, at least in the initial stages of learning. Thus, task complexity must be taken into account as a critical variable in deriving predictions from drive theory with regard to the effects of anxiety (A-State) on motor behavior.

Because of the difficulty in determining the relative strengths of correct responses and competing error tendencies on motor tasks, Martens (1971) concluded that alternative theoretical approaches to drive theory should be pursued. Similarly, Carron (1971) states that "the habit hierarchy in almost all motor tasks is virtually impossible to assess (p. 186)," and gives this as a major reason for advocating that drive theory be abandoned. In his endorsement of Easterbrook's (1959) cue utilization concept as an alternative to drive theory, Martens suggests that task complexity could be defined in terms of the number of task relevant and irrelevant cues that were available to *S*. He notes, however, that specifying the range of cues in a motor task may present the same types of problems as determining the relative strengths of correct and incorrect habits. Indeed, for motor tasks, it would seem more difficult to measure the "cues" that are utilized by *Ss* than to determine the frequency of occurrence of correct and incorrect motor responses.

The other alternative to drive theory suggested by Martens is based on Sarason et al.'s (1960) work with test anxiety. In essence, test anxiety refers to individual differences in anxiety proneness in examination situations, that is, to differences in the tendency to respond with elevations in A-State while taking a test. Persons high in test anxiety ("test A-Trait") are more disposed than low test anxiety *Ss* to experience higher elevations in A-State in situations involving threats to self-esteem imposed by school examinations and other forms of academic evaluation. Thus, test anxiety scales are better predictors of course grades and academic achievement than general anxiety (A-Trait) measures because they are better predictors of elevations in A-State in testing situations.

One might reasonably expect that a measure of anxiety proneness that is specific to a particular motor behavior situation would be a better predictor of A-State and performance in that situation. In competitive swimming, for example, a measure of the disposition to experience elevations in A-State prior to and during a swim meet should be a better predictor of performance than a general anxiety measure such as the MAS or the STAI A-Trait Scale. But in order to predict the effects of differences in A-State on performance, a careful analysis of the essential characteristics of the motor task will be required, along with a theory of motor behavior which specifies the effects of individual differences in A-State or D on performance.

As an alternative to drive theory, Carron (1971) proposes that the effects of stress on learning and performance be examined as a function of individual differences in ability. He logically observes that differences in A-State should have differential effects on performance for Ss who differ in ability. Actually, Carron's approach is quite consistent with drive theory if the theory is extended to include individual differences in ability. We have previously suggested (Spielberger, 1966b) that the strength of the correct and competing response tendencies elicited in verbal learning tasks will be determined by S's intellectual level as well as the intrinsic characteristics of the task. For example, a task of moderate or average difficulty for the general population may evoke relatively few error tendencies in high IQ Ss, but this same task may elicit numerous error tendencies in low-IQ Ss. On such tasks, drive theory would predict that high A-State would facilitate the performance of high-IQ Ss and impair the performance of low-IQ Ss relative to their low anxiety counterparts. Findings consistent with these predictions were reported by Denny (1966) on a concept attainment task, by Katahn (1966) with a maze-learning task, and by Gaudry and Spielberger (1970) in paired-associate learning.

From the foregoing discussion, it will be apparent that clarification of the relationship between anxiety and motor behavior will require (a) a theory of anxiety arousal, and (b) a theory that specifies the effects of individual differences in anxiety on behavior. With regard to the latter, drive theory, with all of its limitations, still appears to provide the most comprehensive explanation of the complex effects of individual differences in anxiety (A-State) on performance.

Applications of drive theory in investigations of motor behavior will require careful evaluation of the response tendencies that are evoked by motor tasks, and this problem is made more difficult by the fact that the relative strengths of correct responses and competing error tendencies change as a function of practice. Furthermore, as Marteniuk (1971) has observed, the effects of variables such as massed and distributed practice and level of arousal during practice must be taken into account. While the problems associated with evaluating the strengths of habits that influence performance on motor learning tasks will be difficult to resolve, these problems will not disappear by simply ignoring them.

Trait-State Anxiety Theory and Motor Behavior

Trait-State Anxiety Theory (Spielberger, 1966a; 1972b) is centrally concerned with anxiety arousal and provides a conceptual framework for classifying the major variables that should be considered in research on anxiety phenomena. In addition to distinguishing between anxiety as a transitory state (A-State) and as a relatively stable personality trait (A-Trait), a comprehensive theory of anxiety must also differentiate between A-States, the stressful environmental conditions or circumstances that evoke these states, and the psychological defenses that serve to avoid or ameliorate them. Another major task for Trait-State Anxiety Theory is to identify the characteristics of stressful situations that evoke differential levels of A-State in Ss who differ in A-Trait.

With regard to the situational stresses that evoke differential A-State reactions, Atkinson (1964) suggests that a "fear of failure" motive is reflected in measures of A-Trait while Sarason (1960) emphasizes the special significance for high A-Trait individuals of failure situations which arouse self-depreciating tendencies. In general, the research literature indicates that situations which pose direct or implied threats to self-esteem produce higher levels of A-State in persons with high A-Trait than in low A-Trait Ss. Research findings also show that high A-Trait Ss tend to do more poorly than Ss who are low in A-Trait under conditions that involve failure or negative evaluation of performance (Spence & Spence, 1966).

Two important classes of stressor situations can be identified that appear to have different implications for the evocation of A-State in Ss who differ in A-Trait: (1) Ss with high A-Trait appear to interpret circumstances in which their personal adequacy is evaluated as more threatening than do low A-Trait Ss; (2) Situations characterized by physical danger are *not* interpreted as differentially threatening by high and low A-Trait Ss. Accordingly, differential elevations in A-State would be expected for Ss who differ in A-Trait under circumstances characterized by some threat to self-esteem, but not in situations that involve physical danger unless personal adequacy is also threatened.

A difficult task, such as an advanced course in mathematics or physics, or one requiring complex motor skills and coordination, might tend to evoke high levels of A-State in most high A-Trait Ss. However, such tasks are not likely to be regarded as threatening by a person with high A-Trait who has the requisite skills and background to do well in them. On the other hand, a recreational course in physical education (tennis, swimming) that most students find interesting and enjoyable might be very threatening to a particular low A-Trait S for whom the course has special traumatic significance. Thus, while measures of A-Trait provide useful information regarding the *probability* that high levels of A-State will be aroused, the impact of any given situation on a particular S can be best ascertained by taking actual measurements of A-State in that situation.

In summary, the principal assumptions of Trait-State Anxiety Theory with regard to the arousal of A-States may be briefly stated as follows:

1. In situations that are appraised by an S as threatening, an A-State reaction will be evoked. Through sensory and cognitive feedback mechanisms, high levels of A-State will be experienced as unpleasant.

2. The intensity of an A-State reaction will be proportional to the amount of threat that the situation poses for S. The duration of an A-State reaction will depend upon the persistence of S's interpretation or appraisal of the situation as threatening.

3. High A-Trait Ss will perceive situations or circumstances that involve threats to self esteem, such as failure or negative evaluation of performance, as more threatening than will Ss who are low in A-Trait, and will respond to such situations with greater elevations in A-State.

4. Elevations in A-State have motivational or drive properties that may directly influence behavior, or serve to initiate psychological defenses that have been effective in reducing A-States in the past.

With regard to the origin of individual differences in A-Trait, it is assumed that residues of past experience dispose high A-Trait Ss to appraise situations that involve some form of personal evaluation as more threatening than do Ss who are low in A-Trait. We may speculate the childhood experiences interact with constitutional (hereditary) factors to influence the development of individual differences in A-Trait, and that parent-child relationships centering around punishment are especially important. The fact that self-depreciating attitudes are aroused in high A-Trait Ss under circumstances characterized by failure or negative feedback suggests that these Ss received excessive criticism and negative appraisal from their parents.

The future of research on anxiety and motor behavior would seem to depe upon the development of appropriate motor tasks in which it is possible to assess the relative strength of correct and competing tendencies. By now, it should also be abundantly clear that, in investigations of the effects of stress on motor behavior, measures of A-State should be obtained in the experimen situation. Finally, since general A-Trait measures have not proved too effectiv in predicting changes in motor behavior, it might be desirable to develop A-Trait measures that are designed to assess individual differences in the disposi to respond with differential A-State reactions in motor behavior situations.

Summary

It is a fact that research using drive theory has not revealed consistent relationships between persons differing in A-trait and motor behavior. This is true when subjects have performed either in apparently threatening or nonthreatening situations. The need for methodological improvements is apparent from a review of this literature.

I criticized drive theory and the MAS as a measure of drive not only on the basis of a failure to reveal consistent findings, but more importantly because it cannot adequately be operationalized for research with complex motor behavior, the type of behavior we find in sport. That is, we do not know enough about complex motor behavior to establish response hierarchies.

Moreover, as Spielberger (1971) points out, his trait-state theory of anxiety is an extension of drive theory if the reactive hypothesis is accepted. Hence, he concurs with Spence that drive theory is still better than any available alternative, but it should be conceptualized within his trait-state paradigm. Spielberger suggests that we need to understand how task difficulty varies for various motor tasks in order to understand the relationship between anxiety and motor behavior. While understanding task difficulty will be useful, it does not appear to be a complete solution. Spence (1971) points out that task difficulty cannot be equated with response dominancy. Thus, we remain where we began: Knowledge of task difficulty will not necessarily permit us to make predictions about response hierarchies with motor tasks.

Spence, Spielberger, and I all concur that better theories of motor behavior are needed. In my effort to assist in this development, I have applauded prodigiously each of my motor learning colleagues whenever they utter words about developments in theories of motor behavior. But as yet, my reinforcements have not given us the theory we need to better understand the anxiety-motor behavior relationship. I have been assured, however, that progress is being made!

I believe the inverted-U hypothesis is a viable alternative to drive theory. In the first reading in this section I specified several reasons for concluding so. My support for the inverted-U hypothesis is not based on what we have already learned, but what appears to be a more viable approach for future study of the relationship between A-trait, arousal, and motor performance. At this time, it appears that the major obstacle thwarting the study of the inverted-U hypothesis is the difficulty in measuring arousal.

REFERENCE NOTES

1. Suinn, R.M. *Visuo-motor behavior rehearsal for athletes.* Paper presented at the National American Psychological Association Convention, New Orleans, August 1974.
2. Rushall, B.S. *The status of personality research and application in sports and physical education.* Paper presented at the Physical Education Forum, Dalhousie University, Halifax, Nova Scotia, January 1972.
3. Morgan, W.P., & Hammer, W.M. *Psychological effect of competitive wrestling.* Paper presented at the American Association for Health, Physical Education, and Recreation, Detroit, April 1971.
4. Gill, D., & Martens, R. *The role of task type and success-failure in group competition.* Manuscript submitted for publication, 1975.
5. Martens, R., & Simon, J. *Competitive trait anxiety as a predictor of pre-competitive state anxiety.* Manuscript submitted for publication, 1976.
6. Gerson, R., & Deshaies, P. *Competitive trait anxiety and performance as predictors of pre-competitive state anxiety.* Manuscript submitted for publication, 1976.

REFERENCES

American Psychological Association. *Standards for educational and psychological tests and manuals.* Washington, D.C.: Author, 1974.

Atkinson, J.W. Motivational determinants of risk-taking behavior. *Psychological Review,* 1957, *64,* 359-372.

Atkinson, J.W. *An introduction to motivation.* Princeton, N.J.: Van Nostrand, 1964.

Atkinson, J.W., & Feather, N.T. *A theory of achievement motivation.* New York: Wiley, 1966.

Berkun, M., Bialek, H., Kern, R., & Yagi, K. Experimental studies of psychological stress in man. *Psychological Monographs General and Applied,* 1962, *76,* 1-39.

Bialer, I. Conceptualization of success and failure in mentally retarded and normal children. *Journal of Personality,* 1961, *29,* 303-320.

Bolles, R.C. *Theory of motivation.* New York: Harper & Row, 1967.

Bowers, K.S. Situationism in psychology: An analysis and a critique. *Psychological Review,* 1973, *80,* 307-336.

Broadhurst, P.L. The interaction of task difficulty and motivation: The Yerkes-Dodson law revived. *Acta Psychologica,* 1959, *16,* 321-338.

Broen, W.E., Jr., & Storms, L.H. A reaction potential ceiling and response decrements in complex situations. *Psychological Review,* 1961, *68,* 405-415.

Carron, A.V. Reactions to anxiety and motor behavior. *Journal of Motor Behavior,* 1971, *3,* 181-188.

Carron, A.V., & Morford, W.R. Anxiety, stress and motor learning. *Perceptual and Motor Skills,* 1968, *27,* 507-511.

Carson, R.C. *Interaction concepts of personality.* Chicago: Aldine Publishing Co., 1969.

Cartwright, D.S. Trait and other sources of variance in the S-R inventory of anxiousness. *Journal of Personality and Social Psychology,* 1975, *32,* 408-414.

Cattell, R.B. *The IPAT anxiety scale.* Champaign, Ill.: Institute for Personality and Ability Testing, 1957.

Cattell, R.B., & Cattell, M.D. *Junior-senior high school personality questionnaire.* Champaign, Ill.: Institute for Personality and Ability Testing, 1969.

Cofer, C.N., & Appley, M.H. *Motivation: Theory and research.* New York: Wiley, 1964.

Cooper, L. Athletics, activity and personality: A review of the literature. *Research Quarterly,* 1969, *40,* 17-22.

Courts, F.A. Relation between muscular tension and performance. *Psychological Bulletin,* 1942, *39,* 347-367.

Denny, J.P. Effect of anxiety and intelligence on concept formation. *Journal of Experimental Psychology,* 1966, *72,* 596-602.

Duffy, E. *Activation and behavior.* New York: Wiley, 1962.

Easterbrook, J.A. The effect of emotion on cue utilization and the organization of behavior. *Psychological Review,* 1959, *66,* 183-201.

Endler, N.S., Hunt, J.M., & Rosenstein, A.J. An S-R inventory of anxiousness. *Psychological Monographs,* 1962, *76,* (Whole No. 536).

Farber, E.I., & Spence, K.W. Complex learning and conditioning as a function of anxiety. *Journal of Experimental Psychology,* 1953, *45,* 120-125.

Fenz, W.D., & Epstein, S. Gradients of physiological arousal of experience and novice parachutists as a function of an approaching jump. *Psychosomatic Medicine,* 1967, *29,* 33-51.

Fenz, W.D., & Jones, G.B. Individual differences in physiologic arousal and performance in sport parachutists. *Psychosomatic Medicine,* 1972, *34,* 1-8.

Fiske, D.W., & Maddi, S.R. *Functions of varied experience.* Homewood, Ill.: Dorsey Press, 1961.

Gaudry, E., & Spielberger, C.D. Anxiety and intelligence in paired-associate learning. *Journal of Educational Psychology,* 1970, *61,* 386-391.

Giambrone, C.P. *The influence of situation criticality and game criticality on basketball freethrow shooting.* Unpublished master's thesis, University of Illinois at Urbana-Champaign, 1973.

Gold, M.A. *A comparison of personality characteristics of professional and college varsity tennis and golf players as measured by the Guilford-Martin personality inventory.* Unpublished master's thesis, University of Maryland, 1955.

Golding, S.L. Flies in the ointment: Methodological problems in the analysis of the percentage of variance due to persons and situations. *Psychological Bulletin,* 1975, *82,* 278-288.

Griffin, M.R. *An analysis of state and trait anxiety experienced in sports competition by women at different ages.* Unpublished doctoral dissertation, Louisiana State University, 1971.

Hardman, K. A dual approach to the study of personality and performance in sport. In H.T.A. Whiting, K. Hardman, L.B. Hendry, & M.G. Jones, *Personality and performance in physical education and sport.* London: H. Kimpton Publishers, 1973.

Harrington, E.F. *Effect of manifest anxiety on performance of a gross motor skill.* Unpublished master's thesis, University of California at Berkeley, 1965.

Husman, B.F. Sport and personality dynamics. In the *Proceedings of the National College of Physical Education Association for Men,* 1969.

Jaspen, N. Serial correlation. *Psychometrika,* 1946, *11,* 23-30.

Johnson, W.R., & Cofer, C.N. Personality dynamics: Psychosocial implications. In W.R. Johnson & E.R. Buskirk (Eds.), *Science and medicine of exericse and sport* (2nd ed.). New York: Harper & Row, 1974.

Johnson, W.R., & Hutton, D.C. Effects of a combative sport upon personality dynamics as measured by a projective test. *Research Quarterly,* 1955, *26,* 49-53.

Johnson, W.R., Hutton, D.C., & Johnson, C.B., Jr. Personality traits of some champion athletes as measured by low projective tests: Rorschach and H-T-P. *Research Quarterly,* 1954, *25,* 484-485.

Katahn, M. Interaction of anxiety and ability in complex learning situations. *Journal of Personality and Social Psychology,* 1966, *3,* 475-479.

Kerlinger, F.N. *Foundations of behavioral research.* New York: Holt, Rinehart & Winston, 1964.

Klavora, P. Emotional arousal in athletics: New considerations. In Mouvement: *Proceedings of the Canadian Psycho-motor Learning and Sport Psychology Symposium,* October 1975.

Kroll, W. Current strategies and problems in personality assessment of athletes. In L.E. Smith (Ed.), *Psychology of motor learning.* Chicago: Athletic Institute, 1970.

Lacey, J., & Lacey, B. Verification and extension of the principle of autonomic response-stereotypy. *American Journal of Psychology,* 1958, *71,* 50-73.

Lazarus, R.S., Deese, J., & Osler, S.J. The effects of psychological stress upon performance. *Psychological Bulletin,* 1952, *49,* 293-317.

Levy, N.A. A short form of the children's manifest anxiety scale. *Child Development,* 1958, *29,* 153-154.

Levitt, E.E. Scientific evaluation of the "lie detector". *Iowa Law Review,* 1955, *40,* 440-458.

Levitt, E.E. *The psychology of anxiety.* New York: Bobbs-Merrill, 1967.

Lowe, R. *Stress, arousal, and task performance of little league baseball players.* Unpublished doctoral dissertation, University of Illinois at Urbana-Champaign, 1973.

Magnusson, D. *Test theory.* Reading, Massachusetts: Addison-Wesley, 1966.

Malmo, R.B. Activation: A neuropsychological dimension. *Psychological Review,* 1959, *66,* 367-386.

Mandler, G., & Sarason, S.B. A study of anxiety and learning. *Journal of Abnormal and Social Psychology,* 1952, *47,* 166-173.

147

Marteniuk, R.G. Two factors to be considered in the design of experiments in anxiety and motor behavior. *Journal of Motor Behavior*, 1971, *2*, 189-192.

Martens, R. Anxiety and motor behavior: A review. *Journal of Motor Behavior*, 1971, *3*, 151-179.

Martens, R. Trait and state anxiety. In W.P. Morgan (Ed.), *Ergogenic aids and muscular performance*. New York: Academic Press, 1972.

Martens, R. *Social psychology and physical activity*. New York: Harper & Row, 1975. (a)

Martens, R. The paradigmatic crisis in American sport personology. *Sportwissenschaft*, 1975, *5*, 9-24. (b)

Martens, R. Competition: In need of a theory. In D.M. Landers (Ed.), *Social problems in athletics*. Urbana, Ill.: University of Illinois Press, 1976.

Martens, R., & Gill, D. State anxiety among successful and unsuccessful competitiors who differ in competitive trait anxiety. *Research Quarterly*, in press.

Martens, R., Gill, D., & Scanlan, T. Competitive trait anxiety and success-failure as related to motor performance. *Perceptual and Motor Skills*, in press.

Martens, R., & Landers, D.M. Motor performance under stress: A test of the inverted-U hypothesis. *Journal of Personality and Social Psychology*, 1970, *16*, 29-37.

Martens, R., & Simon, J.A. Comparison of three predictors of state anxiety when competing. *Research Quarterly*, 1976, *47*, 381-387.

Matarazzo, J.D., Ulett, G.A., & Saslow, G. Human maze performance as a function of increasing levels of anxiety. *Journal of General Psychology*, 1955, *53*, 79-95.

Matarazzo, R., & Matarazzo, J.D. Anxiety level and pursuitmeter performance. *Journal of Consulting Psychology*, 1956, *20*, 70.

McGrath, J.E. A conceptual formulation for research on stress. In J.E. McGrath (Ed.), *Social and psychological factors in stress*. New York: Holt, Rinehart & Winston, 1970.

Mehrabian, A. Male and female scales of tendency to achieve. *Educational and Psychological Measurement*, 1968, *28*, 493-502.

Mellstrom, M., Jr., Cicala, G.A., & Zuckerman, M. General versus specific trait anxiety measures in the prediction of fear of snakes, heights, and darkness. *Journal of Consulting and Clinical Psychology*, 1976, *44*, 83-91.

Mischel, W. *Personality and assessment*. New York: Wiley, 1968.

Mischel, W. Toward a cognitive social learning reconceptualization of personality. *Psychological Review*, 1973, *80*, 252-283.

Morgan, W.P. Pre-match anxiety in a group of college wrestlers. *International Journal of Sport Psychology*, 1970, *1*, 7-13.

148

Morgan, W.P. Hypnosis and muscular performance. In W.P. Morgan (Ed.), *Ergogenic aids in muscular performance*. New York: Academic Press, 1972. (a)

Morgan, W.P. Sport psychology. In R.N. Singer (Ed.), *The psychomotor domain: Movement behaviors*. Philadelphia: Lea & Febiger, 1972. (b)

Nicholson, W.M. The influence of anxiety upon learning: Interference of drive increment? *Journal of Personality*, 1958, *26*, 303-319.

Ogilvie, B.C. Psychological consistencies within the personality of high level competitors. *Journal of the American Medical Association*, 1968, *205*, 156-162.

Oxendine, J.B. Emotional arousal and motor performance. *Quest*, 1970, *13*, 23-32.

Paivio, A., & Lambert, W.E. Measures and correlates of audience anxiety. *Journal of Personality*, 1959, *27*, 1-17.

Rotter, J.B. *Social learning and clinical psychology*. Englewood Cliffs, N.J.: Prentice-Hall, 1954.

Sarason, I.G. Empirical findings and theoretical problems in the use of anxiety scales. *Psychological Bulletin*, 1960, *57*, 403-415.

Sarason, S.B., Davidson, K.S., Lighthall, F.F., Waite, R.R., & Ruebush, B.K. *Anxiety in elementary school children*. New York: Wiley, 1960.

Scanlan, T.K. *The effect of competition trait anxiety and success-failure on the perception of threat in a competitive situation*. Unpublished doctoral dissertation, University of Illinois at Urbana-Champaign, 1975.

Scanlan, T.K., & Passer, M.W. The effects of competition trait anxiety and game win-loss on perceived threat in a natural competitive setting. In R.W. Christina & D.M. Landers (Eds.), *Psychology of motor behavior and sport—1976* (Vol. 2). Champaign, Ill.: Human Kinetics Publishers, 1977.

Scheier, I.J., & Cattell, R.B. *Handbook and test kit for the IPAT 8-Parallel-Form Anxiety Battery*. Champaign, Ill.: Institute for Personality and Ability Testing, 1960.

Simon, J., & Martens, R. SCAT as a predictor of A-states in varying competitive situations. In R.W. Christina & D.M. Landers (Eds.), *Psychology of motor behavior and sport—1976* (Vol. 2). Champaign, Ill.: Human Kinetics Publishers, 1977.

Singh, N.P. Anxiety and sensory-motor learning. *Psychological Studies*, 1968, *13*, 111-114.

Smith, C.P. The origin and expression of achievement-related motives in children. In C.P. Smith (Ed.), *Achievement-related motives in children*. New York: Russell Sage Foundation, 1969.

Spence, J.T. What can you say about a twenty-year old theory that won't die? *Journal of Motor Behavior,* 1971, *3,* 193-203.

Spence, J.T., & Spence, K.W. The motivational components of manifest anxiety: Drive and drive stimuli. In C.D. Spielberger (Ed.), *Anxiety and behavior.* New York: Academic Press, 1966.

Spence, K.W. A theory of emotionally based drive and its relation to performance in simple learning situations. *American Psychologist,* 1958, *13,* 131-141.

Spence, K.W. Anxiety (drive) level and performance in eyelid conditioning. *Psychological Bulletin,* 1964, *61,* 129-139.

Spielberger, C.D. The effects of anxiety on complex learning and academic achievement. In C.D. Spielberger (Ed.), *Anxiety and behavior.* New York: Academic Press, 1966. (a)

Spielberger, C.D. Theory and research on anxiety. In C.D. Spielberger (Ed.), *Anxiety and behavior.* New York: Academic Press, 1966. (b)

Spielberger, C.D. Trait-state anxiety and motor behavior. *Journal of Motor Behavior,* 1971, *3,* 265-279.

Spielberger, C.D. Anxiety as an emotional state. In C.D. Spielberger (Ed.), *Current trends in theory and research* (Vol. 2). New York: Academic Press, 1972. (a)

Spielberger, C.D. Conceptual and methodological issues in anxiety research. In C.D. Spielberger (Ed.),*Current trends in theory and research* (Vol. 1). New York: Academic Press, 1972. (b)

Spielberger, C.D. *State-trait anxiety inventory for children: Preliminary manual.* Palo Alto, Calif.: Consulting Psychologists Press, 1973.

Spielberger, C.D., Gorsuch, R.L., & Lushene, R.E. *Manual for the state-trait anxiety inventory.* Palo Alto, Calif.: Consulting Psychologists Press, 1970.

Spielberger, C.D., & Smith, L.H. Anxiety (drive), stress, and serial-position effects in serial-verbal learning. *Journal of Experimental Psychology,* 1966, *72,* 589-595.

Taylor, J.A. A personality scale of manifest anxiety. *Journal of Abnormal and Social Psychology,* 1953, *48,* 285-290.

Thayer, R.E. Measurement of activation through self-report. *Psychological Reports,* 1967, *20,* 663-678.

Thayer, R.E. Activation states as assessed by verbal report and four psycho-physiological variables. *Psychophysiology,* 1970, *7,* 86-94.

Vale, J.W., & Vale, C.A. Individual differences and general laws in psychology: A reconciliation. *American Psychologist,* 1969, *24,* 1093-1108.

Watson, D., & Friend, R. Measurement of social-evaluative anxiety. *Journal of Consulting and Clinical Psychology,* 1969, *33,* 448-457.

Weinberg, R.S. Anxiety and motor behavior: A new direction. In R. W. Christina and D.M. Landers (Eds.). *Psychology of motor behavior and sport—1976* (Vol. 2). Champaign, Ill.: Human Kinetics Publishers, 1977.

Wenrich, W.W. *A Primer of behavior modification*. Belmont, Calif.: Brooks/Cole Publishing Co., 1970.

Wittenborn, J.R. *The clinical psychopharmacology of anxiety*. Springfield, Ill.: Charles C. Thomas, 1966.

Wolpe, J., & Lazarus, A.A. *Behavior therapy techinques*. Elmsford, New York: Pergamon, 1966.

Yerkes, R.M., & Dodson, J.D. The relation of strength of stimulus to rapidity of habit-formation. *Journal of Comparative Neurology and Psychology*, 1908, *18*, 459-482.

Zuckerman, M. The development of an affect adjective check list for the measurement of anxiety. *Journal of Consulting Psychology*. 1960, *24*, 457-462.

Zuckerman, M., & Lubin, B. *Bibliography for the multiple affect adjective check list*. San Diego, California: Educational and Industrial Testing Service, 1968.